URBAN POVERTY AND ECONOMIC DEVELOPMENT:
A CASE STUDY OF COSTA RICA

Also by Bruce Herrick

URBAN MIGRATION AND ECONOMIC DEVELOPMENT
IN CHILE
ECONOMIC DEVELOPMENT
(with Charles P. Kindleberger)

URBAN POVERTY AND ECONOMIC DEVELOPMENT: A CASE STUDY OF COSTA RICA

Bruce Herrick and Barclay Hudson

St. Martin's Press
New York

All rights reserved. For information, write:
St. Martin's Press Inc., 175 Fifth Avenue, New York, NY 10010
Printed in Hong Kong
First published in the United States of America in 1981

ISBN 0-312-83459-4

Library of Congress Cataloging in Publication Data

Herrick, Bruce H
Urban poverty and economic development.

Includes bibliographical references and index.
1. Poor – Costa Rica.   2. Costa Rica – Social
conditions.   3. Urbanization – Costa Rica.   I. Hudson, Barclay, joint author.   II. Title.
HC143.Z9P624   1980   339.2'2'097286   79-29713
ISBN 0-312-83459-4

Contents

v

List of Tables

List of Figures

List of Maps .

Preface

Performing research on urban poverty exposes analysts to intellectual challenges of a high order. Some satisfaction can be gained by novel approaches that question the received wisdom in the field. Equally rewarding are the personal relations that have characterised our research. The numbers of people involved, especially at the early stages, and the intensity of their shared interest in the subject created a stimulating environment in which our inquiries proceeded.

We want to acknowledge with appreciation the contributions of a study team, assembled by the Costa Rican Office of Planning and Economic Policy (OFIPLAN), whose members were Vinicio Gonzalez, Ignacio Ardid, Anna Porras, Emilia Rodriguez, and Carlos Silva. Some early parts of the research were carried out under a contract financed by the United States Agency for International Development and administered by Practical Concepts Inc of Washington, D.C. The cooperation and support of Fernando Zumbado, Carlos Raabe, Guido Bonilla, Carlos Montero, Hernán Gutierrez, Marisa Pimenta, Rodolfo Tacsan, Esteban Lederman, Edward Butler, Eric Chetwynd, William Miner, and Joe Sconce also pushed the research in productive directions. Some of the conclusions have been aired at conferences and seminars in San José, Costa Rica, and Coventry and Oxford, England. The comments of Biswajit Bannerjee, John Knight, and Ashwani Asaith were especially helpful. Finally, the support of Keith Griffin was crucial to the study's completion.

Readers will recognise without much difficulty that the conclusions we draw are our own and ought not to be interpreted as reflecting the official position of any government or any agency, since in fact, they do not.

Oxford and Santa Monica   BRUCE HERRICK
June 1979   BARCLAY HUDSON

1 Introduction

Poverty is as old as mankind. Organised attempts to alleviate it are more modern. Since World War II, those efforts have often been launched at national and international levels. This book deals with poverty and the problems of large-scale attempts to help poor people. Its main thrust explores a potentially serious flaw in traditional strategies of poverty intervention. The central target of programmes is usually seen as a spatially bounded 'poverty area' – a slum or ghetto, a depressed region or an 'underdeveloped' country taken as a unit.

A territorial image of poverty could be appropriate. It may be true that a division between rich and poor sometimes neatly follows such boundaries. Sometimes identity with a place provides the necessary cohesion for joint action on common problems of poverty. Sometimes indeed the causes and consequences of poverty cluster within isolated territorial islands in a larger sea of progress and well being.

But more often it is otherwise. We believe that poverty programmes and poverty analysis deal with circumscribed geographic units mainly for reasons of expediency. Analysts find their data prearranged by administrative boundaries. They function best by looking at one thing at a time: one aspect of poverty, one geographic scale, one mode of analysis, one policy prescription. Similarly, the policy maker and the programme administrator are interested in manageable jurisdictions for action, allowing well defined indicators of success within specified political units.

One can readily sympathise with the tendency to reduce problems to specific geographic dimensions. It seems to allow elegant and effective problem solving. But poverty cannot usually be treated this way, as the present study tries to show. Poverty is one general manifestation of many social processes operating in conjunction. The processes do not all operate on the same scale. Some have their origins in the behaviour of households. Others unfold at the neighbourhood level. Others are found at the scale of an entire city. Urban agglomerations provide the medium for yet

1

other processes that generate or sustain poverty. Still other aspects of poverty can be traced only at a scale of urban–rural linkages, and on the scale of nations, and on the scale of global economic and political forces. All of these processes, and all of these scales of phenomena bear on the causes of poverty. Equally, they all determine the effectiveness and adequacy of strategies for poverty intervention.

This study seeks, first, to describe the multiple spatial dimensions of poverty. It contrasts with the usual treatment of poverty, confined to a single territorial entity. Second, it tries to show that, given the diversity of levels on which poverty operates, similar diversity of analytical approaches is needed. It is not simply a matter of aggregating data to higher levels, or of disaggregating the statistics to lower ones. The shift from one scale to the next involves changes in the quality of the phenomena taking place, and the nature of analytical method must be adapted accordingly. Survey instruments must be used on some aspects of poverty, census data on others, participant observation, informed judgement, applied theory, ecological systems modelling, concepts of cultural and political behaviour, historical analysis of past social mobilisation strategies – any or all of these may be required, each as a necessary context for the others.

Third, it asks how to make all this practical. Poverty intervention is already an ambitious challenge for policy analysts and social scientists. If we were to insist that poverty analysis discard the convenient illusion of 'solving' poverty on a single level of intervention, might this not make analysis hopelessly complex and intractable? Is it politically realistic to hope to forge a united front of projects and policies operating simultaneously at several levels? And what about the experience of poverty intervention in the past – is any more conceptualising necessary when we have success stories from the past to point the way?

Our response comes from looking at those very success stories. There are not very many of them. The prominent ones in fact do testify to the existence of policies, or at least favourable circumstances, operating on a wide variety of levels, as just suggested. Without attempting to prove the point at any length, one could also look at the numbers of policies and millions of dollars that have been lavished on unsuccessful solutions to poverty, through strategies aimed at a single level of intervention. The record is not very promising. The ILO reports that absolute levels of poverty are worse for a substantial population in some countries which have successfully participated in the 'green revolution'. Although yields per hectare have risen dramatically, commercial production for export has tended to displace local food crops.[1] In Africa, food production per capita declined in twenty-nine countries over the half-decade 1970–75.[2]

We conclude that analytical approaches are required that treat poverty as *a composite phenomenon operating on a range of spatial levels*. The implications for social science parallel the lessons for policy making. One implication points to the need for greater use of available short-cut methods for policy analysis.[3] A second emphasises systematic review of successful past efforts at poverty intervention within a particular region or locality. Past successes like past mistakes tend to be sadly neglected as signposts for the future. Social scientists and politicians alike seem to have little interest in historical memory, or the richness of understanding that comes from historical methods. Yet the history of successful social efforts in a particular place is perhaps the best single test of what it would take to bring about significant changes. This principle operates with special vigour where changes involve complementary policies, or fortuitous conditions of success, operating simultaneously at both finer-grain and larger-scale levels.

A third implication focuses on a strategy of inductive thinking. To social scientists reflexively conditioned to a deductive mode of thought, induction will seem to be 'working backwards'. It does not start from abstract analysis about the nature of poverty and deduce appropriate strategies from those abstractions, but instead builds on concrete initiatives already underway. The idea entails subjecting actual programmes to a systematic but relatively brief critical analysis of multi-scale spatial processes that are helping or hindering their full potential for success. This binds the analysis tightly to concrete realities and keeps it focused on the practical questions of policy implications stemming from the theory or data at hand.

Planning has sometimes been conceived as the mutual interplay between systematic knowledge and organised action. The notion of structuring poverty analysis around the systematic evaluation of significant efforts already underway would take a step closer to this broad ideal of planning. This demands something different of social scientists who are traditionally interested in developing new concepts, or proving old theories, or arriving at abstract 'truths'. It calls for application of knowledge to specific scenarios of problem solving. It also demands something different from politicians who are looking for short-term solutions, or the establishment of programmes and totally fresh starts. It calls instead for steady commitment to difficult and complex solutions that transcend political boundaries.

There is no help for it. The difficulties cannot be avoided. The problem of poverty will not adapt itself to traditions of social science and politics. It will have to be the other way around. This study cannot make that approach much more attractive, but it can help illustrate the need for it, and the feasibility.

A CASE STUDY: COSTA RICA

Most of the data and findings of this book are drawn from Costa Rica. We address ourselves, in part, to people interested in foreign aid and in overseas technical assistance. Reference to a single Central American country can also be useful to people interested in the periodic wars on poverty attempted in the United States and other industrialised nations. Beginning with an entire country means that the study is addressed to policies that are significant at a national scale, and not simply limited to pilot projects. At the same time, seeing how poverty operates in Costa Rica helps us to stand back a little from the conventional ways in which most of us think about poverty. It can serve to cast poverty in a fresh perspective, removed enough from familiar circumstances to be seen as a whole. With that as a starting point, it will be easier to grasp the multiple scales of poverty phenomena that operate both within and beyond the boundaries of the national unit itself.

The choice of Costa Rica as a case study reflects several considerations. In many ways the country displays typical problems of poverty found among other less developed countries. At the same time, by many social indicators it is relatively advanced. In this sense, it serves as a benchmark to the problems and opportunities that many other countries will encounter in pursuing a similar path of development.

The Costa Rican path also calls attention to facets of the development process that go beyond traditional economic indicators. It reminds us that poverty has social and political dimensions as well as economic ones. Costa Rica is widely and justifiably regarded as a model democracy, a rare jewel in a part of the world where few governments have been democratically elected and have served out their terms. Since 1948, elections in Costa Rica have been scrupulously supervised by the judicial branch of government. The country's constitution renounces the maintenance of a standing army. There is a free press and vocal, responsible opposition parties. In the last thirty years, the country has enacted extensive social legislation aimed at assisting poor groups, including universal provision of services in health and education, and family income assistance. The government has also sponsored progressive experiments in areas such as nutrition, housing, and land reform.

From an analytical standpoint, Costa Rica presents a very favourable study area, given the wealth of data collected by its various statistical and service agencies. A good deal of local analysis has been generated by the country's universities, government bureaus, and independent research agencies, and by scholars from abroad. As a host country for foreign aid from many international agencies, Costa Rica has also been the object of study by foreign professionals. From the standpoint of North American interests, Costa Rica has strong import and export ties with the United States, good political relations, and open arms to a growing community of Americans who have brought themselves, their money, and their cultural influence there in search of pleasant retirement living.

SPATIAL DIMENSIONS OF POVERTY IN COSTA RICA

The available data on Costa Rica lead us to the conclusion that poverty is not basically a ghetto phenomenon. It is not spatially circumscribed. It is not a matter of processes operating within distinct territorial units, either at the level of neighbourhoods, or cities, or the country as a whole. Aspects of poverty manifest themselves at each of these levels, but as an overall phenomenon, analysis of poverty cannot be confined to particular spatial units, either in searching for causes or effects.

The data on Costa Rica show this with exceptional clarity. Poor and rich are found mixed together, whether one examines data from the national level, the officially designated Urban Agglomeration in the central plateau, the Metropolitan Area of

San José, or districts and census tracts within the capital city itself. To be sure, there are *tugurios*, or slums, that are geographically well defined, but their income profiles are not dramatically different from other urban districts.

The country's success in avoiding severe duality between rich and poor stems from the progressive social structure and government programmes of Costa Rica. At the same time, continuing poverty poses a challenge to analysts and programmers of technical assistance and service delivery agencies in the field. The poor are there, and many are truly poor, but they are hard to find and reach. In recent decades, the lowest two income deciles gained less than the upper deciles, in relative as well as absolute terms, and the poorest 10 per cent as a group has not made significant gains from the otherwise quite impressive development of Costa Rica's economy and outreach of social services.

An important policy implication follows from these observations. The country's very success in avoiding a divided society with geographical separation between rich and poor means that poverty intervention strategies must be applicable to poor persons no matter where they live, rather than being directed at obvious slum concentrations.

Poverty continues to exist in Costa Rica, and Costa Ricans are well prepared to recognise the distance still to be covered. Poverty, including some truly desperate levels, clearly manifests itself, but a clear picture of its scale and nature is blurred by the use of data averages, whether looking at the national picture, the Metropolitan Area of San José, or the individual slum neighbourhood. To a remarkable degree, the poor do not emerge as second-class citizens in a dual society. This creates problems in identifying and locating them. It masks the scale of the problem. It glosses over the depths of misery that impoverished families experience in their daily lives. It may also open up new opportunities, however, for integrating the poor into the mainstream of development.

Some of these conclusions are drawn from a 1977 empirical study focused on San José's *tugurios*. While poverty was somewhat more concentrated in these slums, shacks, and shantytowns than elsewhere, there remained a broad similarity between many of the socio-economic characteristics of the residents of *tugurios* and those of people living outside these physically deteriorated neighbourhoods. Just as significant, a majority of the city's poor –

three-quarters of them – in fact lived outside the *tugurios*. Poverty in Costa Rica was therefore wider than would be revealed by a study confined to *tugurio* conditions.

Empirical observations showed a number of forms of urban poverty, some associated with particular spatial entities, others not. Most of the poor were able-bodied, unemployed or underemployed and seeking work, and unskilled or semi-skilled but willing to be further trained. Other forms of poverty, however, seemed less distinctly tied to unemployment or low wages. In the most desperate cases, found at the lowest income levels, labour market activities were simply not contemplated. These were persons too old, or too sick, or suffering from emotional problems or alcoholism, or women without husbands and with too many children, or persons otherwise basically disqualified from active labour force participation.

Some factors operate on a larger geographic scale than the *tugurio* itself. For example, on a citywide scale, poverty can be described in terms of market instabilities resulting from several obvious sources: construction booms and slumps, seasonal coffee harvesting on the city's periphery, or cycles in export markets for urban industry. Local investment by individuals – for example, the ploughing of personal savings into home improvements or loans to neighbours, or simply keeping up with payments on a sewing machine – may decline if there is uncertainty about a public slum clearance programme, or if questions arise about squatters' rights on open land. Jobs can be lost overnight because of flooding by a river and by the disruption of public transport from home to workplace, or by the opening of a new shopping centre in the suburbs, displacing downtown markets for small storeowners.

At a higher level of urban agglomerations and regional units, a variety of factors affect urban growth, concentration of activities, sprawl, and migration, and they all affect local distribution of wealth and poverty. For example, the Costa Rican data reveal that, contrary to conventional wisdom, rural-to-urban migration was not a direct major cause of urban poverty, because the economic status of migrants was largely equivalent to populations in their destination areas. The causes of migration, however, give clues to causes of poverty that derive from processes at the scale of sub-national regions: market and weather cycles affecting agricultural profits, and national policies affecting the quality and economic viability of rural life such as credit availability, marketing facilities, social infrastructure, cultural amenities, infusion of urban values, or provision of off-season jobs.

Processes at the national and international levels also affect poverty. International trade negotiations among the member countries in the International Coffee Organisation are obvious. The 1973 oil price increases severely affected the Costa Rican economy. Also influential has been the deliberate or unintentional importation of technological change, cultural dependency, and expectations about the standard of living. Foreign aid priorities have probably had some impact. And in Costa Rica, one sees massive conversion of land from one use to another in search of export markets, particularly timber and cattle. Beef production for export has displaced a large part of food crop production, affecting the overall capital intensity of agriculture and the expulsion of rural workers to urban areas, possibly bringing about a lower degree of national self-reliance in growing food for direct consumption.

At each scale of phenomena observed, different sources of data, different analytical methods, different forms of informed judgement, and different sets of conventional or divergent wisdoms are necessary for an understanding of poverty. Costa Rica is interesting not because poverty operates on so many levels there, but because Costa Rican experience so effectively casts doubt on the conventional and simplistic approach to the analysis of poverty – an analysis that crudely identifies poor people with specific spatial zones, and analyses their problems in splendid isolation from geographically larger and smaller sources of poverty. The actual nature of poverty in Costa Rica may be much like poverty elsewhere. An essential difference lies in the possibility that a study of Costa Rica can draw back the veil of misperception about poverty as a spatial entity, contained in a single format of administrative boundaries, analytical units, and conceptual truths.

BASIC POPULATION AND ECONOMIC CHARACTERISTICS OF COSTA RICA

The mid-1977 population of the country was estimated at 2.1 million. At that time, 41 per cent of the population lived in urban areas (against 59 per cent for Latin America as a whole, and a range of 31 to 50 per cent for the five other Central American countries). The World Bank calculated that per capital GNP in 1975 was US $910, slightly below the Latin American average ($1,030), but higher than most other Central American states (Nicaragua $720, Guatemala $650, El Salvador $450, Honduras $340, Panama $1,060).

Most social indicators show Costa Rica to be fairly advanced. It had a birth rate of twenty-nine thousand (against thirty-seven for Latin America), a 2.4 per cent natural rate of increase (against 2.7 per cent for Latin America), a low rate of infant mortality (thirty-eight per thousand live births against seventy-eight), and high life expectancy at birth (sixty-eight years against sixty-two). Under these conditions it would take Costa Rica twenty-nine years to double its population, to about 4 million in the year 2000.[4] For each of these indicators, Costa Rica was the most advanced of the Middle American countries, including Mexico.

However, as later chapters will show, averages on Costa Rica are deceiving. At the median income level, the picture looked favourable. Below that, there were conditions of significant poverty which the Government was committed to attack through a wide variety of means. However, strategies had not been well coordinated, which pointed to the need for a comprehensive analysis of poverty problems as a basis for design of integrated poverty strategies. The present study is intended to help move in this direction.

In the long run, Costa Rican prospects are favourable, as shown by two phenomena. First, its long-run decline in fertility has been the most rapid ever recorded in a Latin American country, and at the time of writing, it is still falling.[5] The government started to take an active interest in family planning in the mid-1960s, but the decline had already appeared before that time, possibly as a result of other, long-standing government programmes in social services.

The second optimistic sign has been Costa Rica's success in meeting the crisis of oil price increases and general inflation during the mid-1970s. The rate of inflation rose dramatically following the oil crisis. It rose to a peak of 30 per cent per year between 1973 and 1974, but later decline to a more normal 4 per cent in the years immediately thereafter. More to the point, the country's gross domestic product increased at an average annual rate of 6.5

per cent during 1966–77, with inflation held to an average 6 per cent, except for the 1973–5 crisis.

URBAN CENTRES

Like most Latin American countries, Costa Rica has a primate city, San José, located in a pleasant climate on the Central Plateau between mountain ranges running along the northwest–southeast axis of Central America. The term 'San José' can be ambiguous: it can refer to the Central Canton of the capital; to the broader Metropolitan Area; to the Urban Agglomeration as a whole, or to the province which also carries the name San José. In most urban and regional planning documents, however, San José refers to the Metropolitan Area comprising roughly half a million people. The present study focuses principally on this area, and the term 'San José' refers to the greater Metropolitan Area which comprised approximately 500,000 inhabitants in 1973 and 550,000 as of July 1976.[6]

Three smaller cities also lie inside the Central Plateau within a distance of 20 kilometres from the capital: Alajuela (population 34,000), Heredia (26,000), and Cartago (34,000). These and other proximate settlements, along with intervening rural areas, make up a larger region referred to as the Urban Agglomeration, whose total population is on the order of 800,000.

Three other cities deserve note. Puntarenas (population 26,000) on the Pacific coast and Puerto Limón (30,000) on the Caribbean lie at the ends of an east–west axis of cities and roads with its centre in San José. Liberia (11,000) stands by itself in the northwest province of Guanacaste.

Officially, the country is divided into seven provinces which are further sub-divided into cantons and districts. Other units of government are based on geographic areas that do not always coincide with the province–canton–district divisions. At the local level, there are traditional municipalities, whose functions have in some ways been bypassed by the nature and scale of modern urban problems, and eclipsed by new governmental units. Some efforts have been made to renovate and revive government at this level, with help from the government's Institute for Municipal Development (IFAM). There were also other less traditional units at the local level, such as the Community Development Associations. At the country level, the National Planning Office, OFIPLAN, subdivided the country into six planning regions, roughly the size of provinces, but far more logically delineated from the standpoint of territorial integration and policymaking.

The primacy of San José has been considerably stronger than that of capital cities in most other Central American countries, but weaker than found in countries elsewhere in Latin America, where the process of urbanisation is more advanced. Whereas San José contains a quarter of Costa Rica's population, Montevideo contains nearly half of Uruguay's and Buenos Aires more than a third of Argentina's.

The shift of population towards San José from outlying provinces has been viewed by many urban analysts with alarm, and there was continued interest in policies to develop viable growth poles in other regions. The spectres of urban unemployment, crowded housing, pollution, traffic congestion, crime, and other urban ills, have been met with speeches and writings on the need to preserve pride in rural lifestyles, independent farming, preservation of natural resources, and decentralised foci of national life. Other observers have seen the growth of San José as a natural feature of economic and social development, and the inevitable result of coming to the end of agricultural frontiers.

It is simplistic, in any case, to characterise the growth of San José as an urban explosion. Some parts of San José, especially in the Central Canton itself, have shrunk in population, and there were signs that the growth rate had fallen off for the Metropolitan Area as a whole, comparing the 1963–73 decade with the previous one. As in so many other countries, San José has begun a process of suburbanisation, with highest growth rates found roughly five to ten kilometres away from the capital centre.[7]

This spatial description of Costa Rica sets the stage for the more substantive discussion of poverty taken up in subsequent chapters. A number of special topics will be addressed, bearing on different aspects of poverty: income levels, unemployment, migration, social characteristics of the poor, and the organisational resources that serve them; public policies operating on their behalf and technical assistance strategies aimed at poverty intervention. Each topic is presented through Costa Rican data, but description is aimed at illuminating general problems of poverty and opportunities for solutions which have applications elsewhere, both in national development efforts among LDCs and in poverty interventions among more advanced nations.

Throughout the analysis, discussion will revolve around the central theme of the book: poverty as a composite phenomenon operating simultaneously on multiple spatial levels, involving a variety of intersecting processes, and requiring a versatility of analytical approaches to grasp as an integrated system for effective policy intervention.

2 Spatial distribution of population and poverty

LONG-TERM HISTORICAL TRENDS

The Central Plateau of Costa Rica has always been the country's main centre of population, economic activity and government, chiefly because of its favourable climate. In the colonial era, Cartago, near San José, served as the centre of political, ecclesiastical and administrative control. Although power has always remained within the area now designated the Urban Agglomeration, population movements in the country generally have been towards the outer regions, a tendency which was reversed only in the 1960s. There are diverse possible interpretations of the nature and consequences of this new trend towards concentration, but the pattern can be best understood by taking into account the historical processes leading up to the turning point that Costa Rica has experienced.

Table 2.1 shows population growth during the past century and the proportion of population within the Metropolitan Area of San José, within the larger Urban Agglomeration, within the entire Central Valley, and in the rest of the country. It can be seen that maximum concentration in the Agglomeration and Central Valley occurred early in the country's history. Their shares declined steadily with the growth of towns and agricultural activities in the outlying regions. The low point for the Agglomeration was in 1950 (41.1 per cent of total population), while the low point for the Central Valley was in 1963 (55.5 per cent). In the years immediately following, the city centre of San José actually lost inhabitants, from 101,000 in 1963 to 92,000 in 1973. The relative share of this core area had been declining even earlier, from its historical high of 10.9 per cent in 1950 to 4.9 per cent by 1973. The surge of growth in San José was therefore in the outskirts of the Metropolitan Area and in the surrounding belt making up the rest of the Agglomeration. Outside the Agglomeration, growth in

Urban poverty and economic development

TABLE 2.1   Population of Costa Rica and distribution, 1864–1973

	1864	1892	1927	1950	1963	1973
Population (in thousands)						
Costa Rica	120	243	472	801	1336	1872
Central Valley	93	173	282	447	742	1064
Urban Agglomeration*	77	129	197	329	570	854
San José (Metropolitan Area)*	26	46	89	180	321	464
Regions outside Central Valley	27	70	190	354	594	808
Distribution (per cent)						
Costa Rica	100	100	100	100	100	100
Central Valley	77.3	71.1	59.8	55.8	55.5	56.8
Urban Agglomeration*	63.7	52.9	41.9	41.1	42.6	45.7
San José (Metropolitan Area)*	22.0	19.0	18.9	22.5	24.0	24.8
Regions outside Central Valley.	22.7	28.9	40.2	44.2	44.5	43.2

*The boundaries of these geographic units are drawn somewhat differently from other sources used in this study, but the general pattern of population distribution is not greatly affected.

SOURCE
Adapted from Fernando Zumbado and Lydia B. Neuhauser, 'Evolución de la Distribución de la Población en Costa Rica', in Manuel J. Carvajal (ed.), *Políticas de Crecimiento Urbano* (San José, Dirección de Estadísticas y Censos, 1977) tables 2.1 and 2.2, pp. 71, 73.

the Central Valley was slow, more or less keeping pace with population growth in the country as a whole. Fastest growth occurred at places about five to ten kilometres from the city centre.

The previous data present a classic picture of suburbanisation but more careful study would be needed to verify whether this evolution conforms in every detail to the typical syndrome of suburban growth problems such as traffic congestion, decline of the commercial core, and land speculation benefiting a few at the expense of many. Clearly, there has not been a major effort to design urban land uses in the best way for linking residence and work, commerce and entertainment. And just as clearly, suburbanisation is leading to rapid growth of middle-class ghettos at the margin of the city, whose isolation from the centre is made

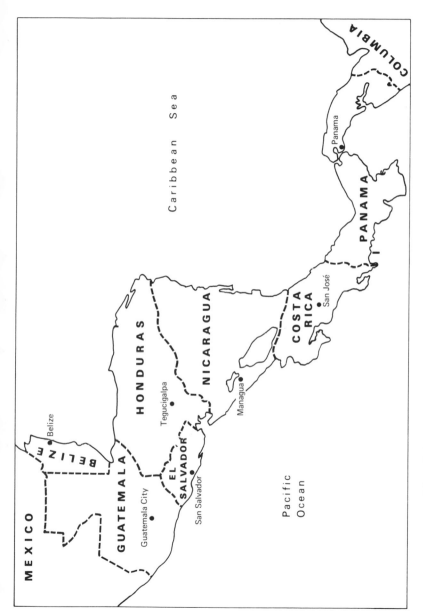

MAP 2.1   Central America – national boundaries and capital cities

15

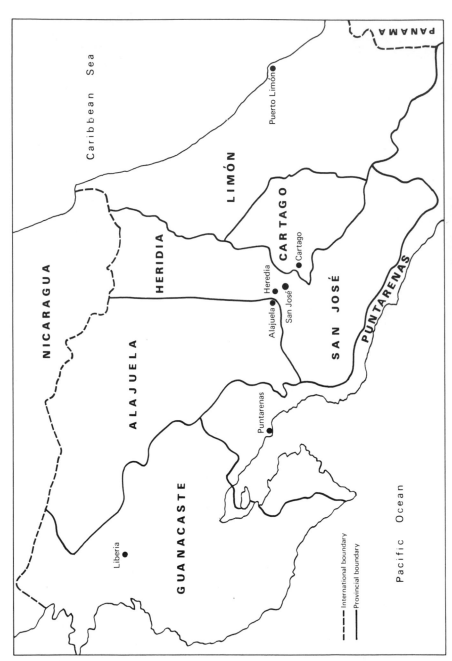

MAP 2.2 Costa Rica: provinces and major cities

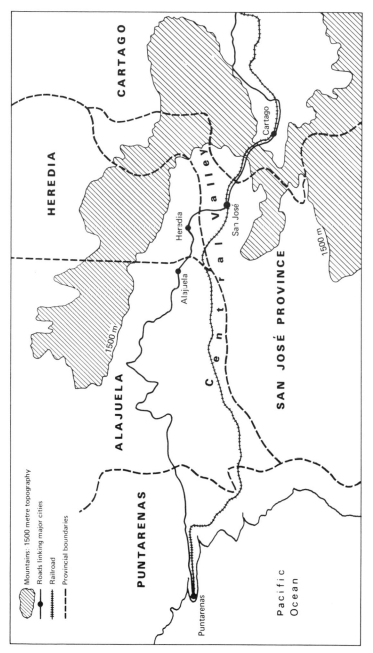

MAP 2.3   Costa Rica – Central Valley, containing the Urban Agglomeration

possible by increasing numbers of private cars and the widening of radial traffic arteries to accompany the growing swarms of commuters.

HISTORICAL FORCES SHAPING THE GROWTH OF SAN JOSÉ

Costa Rica's first official population census was taken in 1864. As shown in Table 2.1, there was already at that time a steady shift in Costa Rican population toward the periphery, outside of San José and beyond the Central Valley. Some of this represented independent farmers, which Costa Rican historical sources frequently cite in explanation of the country's long tradition of democracy, progressive politics and respect for human rights. Frontiers were also pushed back by more commercialised, large-scale agriculture, chiefly in coffee, bananas, cattle and timber, often in foreign holdings, and generally geared to export markets. Coffee harvesting is relatively labour intensive, but recent conversion of farm land to cattle raising is sometimes cited as contributing to rural population expulsion and migration to cities, although as yet there has apparently been no careful study of these facts or cause–effect relationships.[1] Available data indicate that, despite Costa Rica's historical pride in its independent frontiersmen and farmers, its concentration of landholdings does not differ much from the average in other Latin American countries. As will be shown in a later chapter, this is also true for Costa Rica's distribution of wealth.

Apart from rural expulsion, the exhaustion of the agricultural frontier, and problems of erosion and depletion of land from exploitive agricultural practices, a number of other factors bear on the shift in direction of net population growth towards San José.

1 The growth of jobs in San José

New employment is found particularly in the fast-growing industry, construction, and government service sectors. Some of the new jobs may be transitory, or displacing other jobs. Some may be in relatively capital-intensive industries whose long-run effect will be to reduce the net demand for labour. Nevertheless, while the economy continued its present rate of vigorous growth, San José attracted new workers by opening new doors in well-publicised sectors, even if old doors were quietly closing within the same region.

2 Limited decentralisation of industrial investment outside the capital region

Industrial location is often considered the key to regional decentralisation policies. However, growth pole strategies are not built on factories alone, and regional planners are beginning to question the benefits and feasibility of traditional growth pole policies. This is discussed further in chapter 8.

3 Climate

The favourable climate that brought the first colonists to the Central Plateau has continued to attract people who can make a free choice of residential and business location.

4 Markets, commerce and communication

Costa Rica is not a large country, and San José is the only large concentrated outlet for goods produced for domestic consumption. The capital is centrally located, and strategically placed in the middle of the east–west axis of smaller cities running from the Caribbean to the Pacific. It is also the centre of gravity for three of the country's five secondary cities with 20–30,000 population size. San José's international airport has taken over many of the international freight functions previously handled by the port city of Puntarenas. The three maps shown earlier in this chapter illustrate the central role of San José in regard to the country's network of commerce.

5 Culture

One attraction of San José is the range of facilities that only a large city can support. In part, San José has symbolic attributes, such as the National Theater, which have special appeal to a small but important class of people with money and influence, who constitute at the same time an important pool of entrepreneurship for development activities. In part, San José exerts a cultural impact through its European and North American characteristics, which are in turn beamed out to the provinces through public and private media.

6 Government centralisation

Decisions, administrative facilities, political influence, and routes to success have traditionally been located in the capital, reflecting the Spanish colonial heritage of primate cities. In the recent rapid growth of Costa Rican government activities, many functions have been delegated to autonomous agencies outside the central government, although their headquarters have remained in San José.

7 Specialised services

The capital is a natural location for one-of-a-kind facilities in areas such as specialised medicine, technical assistance, central bank functions, data processing, and other activities, especially those that draw upon agglomerations of other skills and activities.

Traditional functional analysis of an urban system gives less attention than deserved to questions of climate, culture, and service amenities. Better data are generally available on economic factors and their direct influence is more easily measured. Before discussing further the factors working towards concentration in San José, it is useful to list briefly some of the countervailing forces that might be operating to make the periphery more attractive.

COUNTERVAILING FORCES TOWARDS THE PERIPHERY

1 Reverse migration

Most data on population movements show changes from one year or decade to the next, but such figures are based on a netting-out of migration moving in both directions. Reverse migration may vary according to individual motivations and personal circumstances, or more general historical forces. Some factors may be within the control of public policy, such as relative growth in employment and unemployment rates, housing and education facilities. As described in Chapter 3, the causes of migration still are not well understood, although several studies have been undertaken on the subject using Costa Rican data.[2]

2 Enriched infrastructure of small outlying cities

Fox and Huguet have pointed out that, compared with other Latin American countries, Costa Rica's rural towns have an unusually 'urban' character.[3] Small towns do not serve as agricultural villages to the extent that they do in Mexico or in neighbouring Nicaragua, where roughly 30 to 70 per cent of the male labour force works in the fields. In Costa Rica, towns under 10,000 population designated 'urban' have only 14 per cent of the economically active population in agriculture.

3 Provision of basic services outside San José

Education and health facilities extend well into the periphery, reflected in high levels of literacy, life expectancy and infant

TABLE 2.2   Percentage of formal illiteracy, 1892–1973, by province*

Provinces	1892	1927	1950	1963	1973
Costa Rica	71.8	34.2	21.2	14.3	10.9
San José	62.9	29.8	15.6	10.0	7.0
Alajuela	78.4	35.8	23.5	15.2	11.4
Cartago	78.9	40.3	23.4	14.7	11.4
Heredia	68.2	24.5	11.7	8.3	6.0
Guanacaste	78.2	43.5	32.5	20.2	15.8
Puntarenas	79.3	51.1	29.1	23.3	18.8
Limón	63.2	22.9	20.2	18.2	17.8

NOTE
*Estimates based on population over 10 years old.

SOURCE
Adapted from census data.

survival. Zumbado and Neuhauser have noted cases of migration flows towards rural cantons with inferior provision of basic services,[4] so caution is needed in building a policy of population decentralisation around the attractive power of investment in service amenities.

Significant gaps between urban and rural services still exist, but many are being closed, as illustrated by the data in Tables 2.2 and 2.3 on literacy, and drinking water facilities.

TABLE 2.3   Percentage of population supplied with drinkable water

Means of supply	1967 Urban	1967 Rural	1969 Urban	1969 Rural	1972 Urban	1972 Rural
Aqueduct	100.0	49.6	100.0	55.0	100.0	65.0
Household outlet	89.8	34.1	92.4	38.5	95.0	56.0

SOURCE
Servicio Nacional de Acueductos y Alcantarillado.

4 Land use

Much has been written about the exhaustion of the agricultural frontier, but the problem is probably not so much in the lack of total space available as in its use. The situation in Costa Rica might be compared to England's eighteenth-century experience with the enclosure movement that sent waves of uprooted people to the city, or the US experience with the dust bowl in the 1930s. It has not yet come to that in Costa Rica, but the potential is there: no agency is yet taking full responsibility for agricultural practices that might lead to major social and ecological problems, and symptoms of those phenomena are visible. Some choices are clear: whether to use land in extensive holdings, using capital intensive methods, and producing for export; or whether to encourage intensive methods using less land and more labour. Presently, the choice is decided by markets, and more deliberate intervention would require a mixture of price supports, technical assistance, redistribution of land rights, provision of credit facilities and other familiar strategies of rural development.

INDUSTRIAL LOCATION AS A FACTOR IN THE HEGEMONY OF SAN JOSÉ

Regional decentralisation policies traditionally emphasise the role of industrial location in creating growth poles. Urban and regional analysis is often undertaken with such policies in mind. Strategies of this sort have been attempted in many countries, and past legislation in Costa Rica has followed the conventional path of encouraging industrial parks in outlying regions.[5] There are, however, a number of issues relating to decentralisation, especially industrial location, which need to be considered.

First, experience elsewhere has shown that the incentives for industry to locate outside of its natural preference tend to be ineffective, or else highly expensive in terms of the explicit or implicit subsidies involved. This varies, of course, by country and industry, and a certain amount probably depends on the cleverness of planners in packaging a wide range of non-monetary incentives, such as amenities, assured markets and sources of supply, urban facilities, pleasant choice of site, political autonomy and wooing of leadership. The attraction of a special regional identity might also be conferred by the presence of a university or sports centre, noteworthy architecture (such as Brasilia offers), or special privileges (for example, free port facilities). This takes place only when planning is combined with extraordinary vision, leadership, and special regional circumstances.

The second problem with growth poles is their vague purpose and their possible ineffectiveness in serving the poor. Growth poles are often prescribed to relieve the central city of 'urban ills' that, on closer look, are mainly problems for the upper and middle classes. Traffic congestion hurts those with cars and those who put a high value on their personal time lost in transit delay. Migration disturbs the middle class which would rather have poverty hidden away in the country where the life of 'simple needs' and 'living off the land' can be rationalised as an accepted norm. Special efforts would need to be made to gear decentralisation towards the problems of the poor.

Analyses of the incidence of benefits flowing from decentralised industrial parks are scarce, but indications are that jobs and profits do not trickle down very far to the lower classes. Profits are quickly repatriated to the capital region or abroad. New factories located in the periphery tend to use modern, capital-intensive methods, requiring higher skill levels drawn from better-off population groups. Tracing the long run consequences of growth pole investments is difficult owing not only to the many factors involved and the extended time frame, but also to the diversity of theoretical interpretations of the data used to trace linkages. Earlier theories depicting growth poles as engines of regional development are confronted with more recent theories which construe them as mere extensions of traditional centralised firms whose major role has been to exploit the rural sector for the benefit of the rural rich, urban parent companies, multinational interests, and foreign markets. Arguments on each side have been thrashed out in numerous publications and international planning conferences without consensus. Whatever the substantive merits of the pessimistic view, it does tend to emphasise issues of the *incidence* of costs and benefits. In any case, developments in the field of growth pole theory deserve close watch, especially with regard to their role in serving the distinctive needs of the poor.[6]

The third and final problem of using industrial location as a catalyst for growth in peripheral regions is that industrialisation is not necessarily the best investment. Forward and backward economic linkages of industry in isolated settings tend to be limited, given reduced markets for factory-produced goods on the one hand, and undeveloped sources of supply on the other. It is generally true that multiplier and accelerator effects of new investment are small within narrow geographic units. Zumbado and Neuhauser[7] state that industry in Costa Rica is heavily dependent on materials and components that are imported, and that interindustry linkages are fairly weak. Outside of San José considerable investment has gone into agro-industry; but there is also a substantial portion of agro-industry located within San José, including more than 40 per cent of food, beverage and tobacco establishments.

Industrial employment in Costa Rica grew steadily, but relatively slowly, surpassed by every other sector except agriculture and energy over the period 1950–73 (see Table 2.4). Industry offered employment to 11.0 per cent of the active labour force in 1950, 11.5 per cent in 1963 and 11.9 per cent in 1973. As of 1973, the faster-growing service sector was offering nearly twice as many jobs as industry (132,000 against 69,000), with commerce (67,000) also overtaking industry, and transportation (24,000) and construction (39,000) also growing at a faster pace. The potential

TABLE 2.4 Economically active population by economic sector, 1950–73

Economic sector	Numbers			Percentage			Average annual rate of increase (percentages)		
	1950	1963	1973	1950	1963	1973	1950-63	1963-73	1950-73
Total	271,984	395,273	585,313	100.0	100.0	100.0	2.9	4.0	3.4
Farming	148,837	194,309	213,226	54.7	49.1	36.4	2.1	0.9	1.6
Mining	754	1,127	1,557	0.3	0.3	0.3	3.1	3.3	3.2
Industry	29,870	45,332	69,917	11.0	11.5	11.9	3.3	4.4	3.8
Commerce	21,412	38,660	67,675	7.9	9.8	11.6	4.6	5.8	5.1
Transportation	9,465	14,738	24,964	3.5	3.7	4.3	3.5	5.4	4.3
Construction	11,625	23,304	39,078	4.2	5.9	6.7	5.5	5.3	5.4
Services	40,166	68,080	132,646	14.8	17.2	22.7	4.1	6.9	5.3
Energy	1,607	4,215	5,531	0.6	1.1	0.9	7.7	2.8	5.5
Other	8,248	5,508	30,719	3.0	1.4	5.2	-3.1	18.8	5.9

SOURCE
Fernando Zumbado and Lydia B. Neuhauser, 'Evolución de la Distribución de la Población en Costa Rica', in Manuel J. Carvajal (ed.), *Políticas de Crecimiento Urbano* (San José, Dirección de Estadísticas y Censos, 1977) p. 102.

TABLE 2.5 Average salary (colones per month) and percentage distribution of workers' salaries paid, by economic sector, 1973

Economic sector	Average salary	Less than 200	200-399	400-599	600-799	800-999	1000-1199	1200-1399	1400-1599	1600 and more
Farming	394.8	20.9	46.8	16.7	8.3	3.7	1.5	0.7	0.4	1.0
Mining	562.4	11.7	31.1	32.6	12.1	4.9	1.8	1.1	0.7	4.0
Industry	666.5	9.4	25.5	25.6	13.3	7.7	5.0	3.3	2.5	7.7
Commerce	716.8	9.9	25.6	28.6	12.4	6.6	4.2	2.5	2.1	8.1
Transportation	812.1	10.2	13.2	19.3	19.7	10.6	8.7	5.9	3.6	8.8
Construction	583.6	15.3	24.5	26.9	15.1	7.4	3.5	2.1	1.4	3.8
Financial and Insurance Establishments	1598.1	4.7	8.8	13.4	11.4	9.8	8.8	5.8	5.2	32.1
Community, Social, and Personal Services	1094.0	3.7	7.8	16.4	18.2	12.8	11.2	8.6	5.1	16.2

SOURCE
Zumbado and Neuhauser, op. cit., p. 103.

importance of the construction sector should be seriously considered, especially because of its strong forward and backward linkages and the tradition of lower income group employment, judging from average salaries (see Table 2.5). Also, the relatively high cost of labour in Costa Rica, coupled with the increasing capital intensity of industry, means that special efforts will need to be made to generate new employment opportunities for the poor in the industrial sector. To the extent that the industrial sector cannot generate such employment, the construction sector may offer new opportunities.

Trends in industrial location

More than half of Costa Rica's industrial employment is located in San José Province.[8] A rising number and proportion of industries have received government incentives to decentralise and plan to establish themselves outside San José (see Table 2.6). It is not clear, however, whether they are locating outside the Agglomeration, outside the Metropolitan Area, or simply outside of the San José Central City.

TABLE 2.6   Government incentives for industrial decentralisation

Year	Number of contracts approved	Percentage of contracts approved according to location	
		San José	Outside San José
1972	101	83	17
1973	78	71	29
1974	106	80	20
1975	139	60	40
1976 (up to July)	48	52	48

SOURCE
Bernard Becaux, 'The Industrial Sector in Costa Rica', San José, mimeo, 1977, paragraph 1.25.

SOME POLICY IMPLICATIONS

It is not likely that urban poverty in San José can be alleviated by establishing industrial growth poles in the country's periphery. San

José fills the traditional role of a Latin American primate city. The country's earlier history of population dispersion towards the periphery has reversed itself in recent decades, and the causes of this trend make it virtually unalterable. The century-long expansion into the agricultural frontier has given way to the inexorable forces of modernisation characterised by urban–industrial development. More properly speaking, the picture is one of urban development on the triple base of service–commerce–industry, with a parallel levelling off of agricultural employment, whose growth rate fell from 2.1 per cent in 1950–63 to 0.9 per cent in 1963–73.[2] Present urban population, however, has been shifting from the San José central city towards the outskirts of the Metropolitan Area and the belt of secondary cities making up the Agglomeration. Efforts to refocus development energies into the farther provinces may well benefit those areas, but probably at high cost. It is unlikely that such policies would relieve San José of the more obvious problems of urban growth and suburbanisation, unless they were accompanied by plans that embodied exceptional vision and leadership. Even if planners could count on these factors, however, it might prove more effective to focus on poverty where it exists, rather than attempting the dubious task of intervention through long-term strategies to shift the spatial distribution of urban functions.

Sophisticated theories exist describing optimal spatial distribution of urban functions in ways to better serve the interests of the poor. Nevertheless these require an ideological perspective on urban problems and a commitment to large scale intervention on many fronts that seem impractical in the Costa Rican context. It would seem more straightforward and effective to go directly to the poor communities themselves. This means that decentralisation policies must be directed towards solving the problems of the poor in those areas, not shifting population growth patterns. The rationale for decentralisation would not be to alter urban functions, but to provide new services and opportunities for the rural poor.

In formulating programmes, certain points need to be kept in mind. First, urban poverty programmes have to rely on parallel efforts to improve living conditions in rural areas. Second, migrants often are better educated and motivated than sedentary people; therefore, migration to San José may represent not so much a burden to the Metropolitan Area as a stripping away of skills and initiative from the areas left behind. Third, strategies for community development in urban and rural areas may have much in common, and urban policies need to be developed in light of careful scrutiny of experience gained from past programmes.

Fourth, it is necessary to determine clearly the goals of poverty intervention efforts. Urban and regional analysis often consigns to regional growth poles and the role of lightning rod for the ills of the central Agglomeration. There is not much evidence that such policies are effective, and even less evidence that they help the poor. The energies spent in shifting economic infrastructure from one part of the country where it naturally gravitates to other parts where it resists taking root, might better be invested in direct services to poor communities wherever they are found. The basic needs of poor communities are very evident: housing, employment, education, health provision, nutrition, and a say in their own destinies.

If we seek to provide the poor with jobs and education and houses, the unique contribution of an urban analysis is to point out the need for these to be mutually reinforcing efforts. Housing construction policies can be designed specifically to provide jobs for the poor. If sites and services make more economic sense than houses, but are aesthetically unappealing, public works projects can be generated to remedy this – a park here, a cooperative garden for truck farming there, rows of trees, sports fields, and civic facilities – again with maximum use of labour supplied by the local unemployed. There are precedents for such an approach, and these speak louder than piecemeal projects and grand visions of the Central City Beautiful, or systems of growth poles that leave poverty to be handled elsewhere.

In sum, to the extent that there are insufficient opportunities in the higher productivity industrial sector, logically, priority should be given to self-improvement projects, hiring the poor to provide infrastructure and services that other poor people can afford best. This diverges from the more natural line of urban poverty analysis, which conceives of solutions on a grand scale, through costly but usually futile efforts to reshape the functions and locations of urban activities. It also diverges from the usual strategy of hiring the people who are relatively well off to deliver basic needs to the poor. It means that planners must look beyond industrial location as the catalyst for development of poor communities, whether in the rural periphery or the city slums.

Opportunities in the construction sector also deserve special attention, partially because this sector generally can absorb unskilled labour with more ease (given the proper design of projects); be put to work in physical improvement projects that can overcome some of the demoralising aesthetic failings of *tugurios*; and build up strong forward and backward linkages. Service occupations should also be maximised: they pay better than construction; they presently employ twice the number of workers found in industry; they are continuing to grow quickly; and the majority of service workers (63 per cent in 1973) are in the public sector which is potentially more responsive to national policy than private industry.[10]

3 Urban migration

INTRODUCTION

Urbanisation in Costa Rica as in other low-income countries has drawn increasing attention since the decline in the death rate led to faster rates of population growth. In this research, our particular interested centred in the officially designated San José Metropolitan Area, the situation of the poor who live there, the particular slums and shantytowns (*tugurios*) in which physical deterioration was most evident, and the role of migration.

Popular impressions, reflected in the media and elsewhere, suggest that migrants form a particularly disadvantaged group, with lower incomes and higher unemployment rates than non-migrants and that the problems of urbanisation associated with the growth in number and size of *tugurios* can be traced to the size and rate of the migratory influx. Data from Costa Rica, however, give a quite different picture of migrants and the role they play in urban poverty. In part, the choice of urban boundaries affects the outcome of the analysis. We focused on the so-called Metropolitan Area, rather than the larger Urban Agglomeration which also has been officially recognised. The Metropolitan Area, while it includes the suburbs on the outskirts of San José, does not incorporate the neighbouring provincial capitals of Alajuela, Heredia, and Cartago. As this chapter and its appendix show, the strongest migratory impulses followed a classical pattern of focusing on these neighbouring towns rather than the Metropolitan Area of the national capital itself.

RATES OF MIGRATION

Visual impressions suggested that the number and size of slum neighbourhoods in San José have increased. From this generality, quite plausible interpretations and conclusions have been made,

31

such as:

    I the rat of migration itself was increasing;
   II the Metropolitan Area had become relatively more attractive as a target for migration; and
  III the migrants who arrived 'must be' concentrated in these growing foci of deterioration.

The evidence on the matter, however, did not reinforce these popular beliefs. The rate of population growth attributable to internal migration to San José was constant between the two intercensal periods 1950–63 and 1963–73, and fell thereafter, at least in the *tugurio* neighbourhoods.

Intercensal net migration to San José was measured by Juan Chackiel in his seminar paper, 'Metropolización y cambio demográfico en Costa Rica'.[1] This work discussed population growth for San José and disaggregated it between so-called natural increase (births minus deaths) and net internal migration, all stated in rates per thousand people:

	1950—63	*1963—73*
Birth rate	43	32
Death rate	− 9	− 6
Rate of natural increase	34	26
Net migration rate	+13	+13
Rate of population increase	47	39

The table recites the familiar facts of rapid decline in the birth rate, a simultaneous fall in the death rate by considerably smaller amounts, and a rate of net migration that turned out to be constant.

Thus in the intercensal period ending in 1973, migration accounted for one-third of total population growth in San José. In the previous period, the same *rate* of migration had accounted only for about 28 per cent of population growth. In terms of absolute numbers, of course, a constant *rate* of urban migration implies ever increasing *numbers*, but this falls short of the claims of 'acceleration', which definitionally is an increase in the rate. Such an increase, as the table shows, was not observed.

It may nevertheless be instructive to look at rates of net internal migration in terms of the absolute numbers of persons involved. If the base population in San José were about 194,000 in 1950, then a 1.3 per cent rate of increase attributable to net migration would involve 2,500 migrants. At a later date, say 1973, when the base population was about 500,000, a 1.3 per cent rate implies net immigration amounting to 6,500 (net) migrants per year. Greater numbers of migrants create new and larger demands for housing and social infrastructure. At the same time, since they are concentrated in the young–adult ages, they bring productive capabilities with them that add to the city's human resources.

A 1977 sample survey of adults in the *barrios marginales* provided additional information on the changing rate of migration.[2] Migrant adults were asked when they had arrived. Their responses are summarised as follows:

Date of arrival	Proportion of migrant adults
1913–69	54.2%
1970–73	26.3
1973–77	15.8
No response	3.7
Total:	100.0%

In comparing two periods (1970–73 and 1973–77) of roughly equal length before and after the census date of 1973, the survey showed a fall in the rate of gross immigration. We say 'gross', because we cannot tell from the survey alone how many people left the San José area during the periods in question. Therefore, only inflows were registered. The figures, while not strictly comparable with the rates of net migration cited in the Chackiel study, nevertheless reinforce the notion of an *absence of acceleration* in the rates of urban migration to the San José Metropolitan Area.

MIGRATION AND URBAN POVERTY

Tabulations from the 1973 census related urban migration to San José and the situations of the migrants in two kinds of city neighbourhoods (*tugurios* and non-*tugurios*). For our purposes, 'migrants' were those San José residents who had moved to the capital during the five-year period preceding the census. We ask: are migrants better or worse off than those who have lived in San José for a longer period of time?

Where migrants live in San José

As Table 3.1 shows, migrants made up 21 per cent of the *tugurio* population and 19 per cent outside those neighbourhoods. These simple facts have straightforward implications: first, the proportion of migrants was not as high as some alarmist commentaries might have led one to believe: only about one-fifth of San José's population entered the city during the five years before 1973. While 21 and 19 per cent are certainly not negligible, they are well within the bounds of urban migration found in other Latin American capitals. Second, the proportion of migrants in *tugurios* and outside *tugurios* was similar, differing by only two percentage points. Once again, the popular impression that *tugurios* consisted mainly of recent migrants was clearly contradicted. Migrants were hardly more numerous there than they were in other parts of the city.

Income distribution

Were recent migrants relatively poorer than non-migrants? Again, the answer appears to be, only slightly poorer. While 21 per cent of *tugurio* families were migrants, 23 per cent of the families in the lowest income class in *tugurios* were migrants. Virtually the same relationship existed outside the *tugurios*. The figures, in short, were so nearly equal that the common impression that urban migrants formed a disproportionately underprivileged class is directly contradicted. Both with respect to neighbourhood and with respect to income, the situation of migrants was nearly indistinguishable from that of non-migrants.

Average family size, dependency rate and number of children less than fifteen years old

In city life, larger families, more dependents, and greater number of young children clearly imply barriers to economic betterment.

TABLE 3.1 Number of families by income group

| | Tugurio neighbourhoods | | | | Other neighbourhoods | | | | Total San José | | | |
| | Migrant | | Non-migrant | | Migrant | | Non-migrant | | Migrant | | Non-migrant | |
Annual income level	No.	%	No.	%	No.	%	No.	%	No.	%	No.	%
All income groups	2801	21	10438	79	15127	19	66076	81	17928	19	76514	81
Higher than ₡2000 ($260)	1404	20	5711	80	10400	18	48188	82	11804	18	53899	82
Less than ₡2000	1397	23	4727	77	4727	21	17888	79	6124	21	22615	79
Less than ₡1300 ($170)	827	23	2732	77	2769	22	9685	78	3596	22	12417	78

NOTE
Colones converted at 7.7 per US $1.00. Income levels are per capita. See discussion, chapter 6.

SOURCE
Government of Costa Rica, 1973 Population Census Tapes; special tabulation by University of Florida, Gainesville.

TABLE 3.2 Average family size by income group

Income level	Tugurio neighbourhoods		Other neighbourhoods		Total San José	
	Migrant	Non-migrant	Migrant	Non-migrant	Migrant	Non-migrant
All income groups	5.59	5.56	5.17	5.28	5.24	5.32
Higher than ₡2000 ($260)	4.58	4.82	4.67	4.93	4.65	4.92
Less than ₡2000	6.61	6.45	6.26	6.24	6.34	6.28
Less than ₡1300 ($170)	6.84	6.45	6.13	6.04	6.30	6.13

NOTE
Colones converted at 7.7 per US $1.00.

SOURCE
See Table 3.1.

36

TABLE 3.3 Dependency rate by income group

Income level	Tugurio neighbourhoods		Other neighbourhoods		Total San José	
	Migrant	Non-migrant	Migrant	Non-migrant	Migrant	Non-migrant
All income groups	0.91	0.85	0.75	0.69	0.77	0.71
Higher than ₡2000 ($260)	0.54	0.54	0.55	0.53	0.55	0.53
Less than ₡2000	1.30	1.26	1.21	1.16	1.23	1.18
Less than ₡1300 ($170)	1.55	1.48	1.33	1.31	1.38	1.35

NOTE
Colones converted at 7.7 per US $1.00.

SOURCE
See Table 3.1.

TABLE 3.4 Average number of children under age 15, per family, by income group

Income level	Tugurio neighbourhoods		Other neighbourhoods		Total San José	
	Migrant	Non-migrant	Migrant	Non-migrant	Migrant	Non-migrant
All income groups	2.59	2.37	2.11	1.92	2.18	1.98
Higher than ₡2000 ($260)	1.55	1.53	1.58	1.50	1.57	1.51
Less than ₡2000	3.63	3.39	3.28	3.03	3.36	3.11
Less than ₡1300 ($170)	4.05	3.60	3.33	3.06	3.50	3.18

NOTE
Colones converted at 7.7 per US $1.00.

SOURCE
See Table 3.1.

Did migrants, in *tugurios* and outside of them, labour under these difficulties?

Tables 3.2, 3.3, and 3.4 provide some answers. Migrants at low income levels in *tugurios* did indeed have larger families than non-migrants. In fact, persons at all income levels living in *tugurios* had larger families than those living in the better neighbourhoods. Extended families help to assure continuous income for the family, although not all of the members may be simultaneously earning incomes. Of course, family support systems exist in upper-income families as well, but these families can enjoy the luxury of living in separate houses, rather than in a single residence.

The dependency rate measures the numbers of persons in the so-called dependent ages relative to those in the ages where labour force participation is more customary. For our purposes, the rate is defined as follows:

$$\text{dependency rate} = \frac{\text{No. of persons under 15 and above 64}}{\text{No. of persons between 15 and 64}}$$

The definition overlooks the fact that not everyone under fifteen years of age or over sixty-four is a 'dependent', nor do all those persons between fifteen and sixty-four work in gainful occupations. The dependency rate is, therefore, best interpreted as a strictly demographic variable relating to age composition of the population, rather than having a more profound meaning.

As shown in Table 3.3, low-income families had more dependents than higher-income families. *Tugurio* families had higher dependency ratios, reinforcing the family size observations about them. Also, low-income migrants in *tugurios* had slightly higher ratios than non-migrants. Note, however, that for middle-income groups (those with per capita annual incomes greater than ₡2,000 in 1973), the dependency ratios were nearly equal for migrant and non-migrant families.

Finally, Table 3.4 shows the number of younger children living in each family. Not surprisingly, the lower the income level, the larger the number of younger children – thus reinforcing earlier conclusions relating to family size and dependency ratios.

Age of head of household

Differential ages of household heads can be interpreted in a human capital framework. Assume that, in similarly defined groups,

TABLE 3.5 Average age of head of household, by income group

Income level	Tugurio neighbourhoods		Other neighbourhoods		Total San José	
	Migrant	Non-migrant	Migrant	Non-migrant	Migrant	Non-migrant
All income groups	37.5	42.9	38.8	45.0	38.6	44.7
Higher than ₡2000 ($260)	36.2	43.2	38.1	44.9	37.9	44.7
Less than ₡2000	38.9	42.7	40.2	45.2	39.9	44.7
Less than ₡1300 ($170)	39.9	43.6	41.0	46.3	40.7	45.8

NOTES
Colones converted at 7.7 per US $1.00.

SOURCE
See Table 3.1.

persons entered the labour force at the same age. The older person would have worked longer and would therefore have more on-the-job training. Therefore, within limits, the older the head of household, the more human capital he or she embodies, and the greater his productivity.

These presumptions are completely consistent with the observations reported in Table 3.5. Migrants were younger than non-migrants, reflecting among other things the well known age selectivity of migration. Family heads living in *tugurios* were also younger than those living elsewhere, among both migrants and non-migrants. At least part of *tugurio* poverty, therefore, can be explained by the age distribution of their residents.

Formal educational attainments

Educational attainment presented by far the most puzzling results from the census tabulations. Normally, educational attainment is considered as an embodiment of human capital. Persons with a greater number of years of education, according to this interpretation, would be the bearers of more human capital, would therefore be more productive, and would earn higher incomes than persons who had spent less time in schools.

Observations from the 1973 census, shown in Table 3.6, seem to contradict this 'norm'. It was earlier established that non-migrants have slightly higher incomes than migrants. But migrants had an index of schooling[3] more than double that of non-migrants. In fact, the contrast between the two groups, given their great similarity in other aspects, raises some question about the reliability of these figures. Also, Table 3.6 shows that the lower the income of the non-migrants, the higher their educational level. This is contrary to all expectations relating to education and income levels – and as such leads to further questions on the reliability of the education data.

Both theory and evidence from other countries point to education as a factor associated with upward mobility, which in turn leads to high propensity for migration among the better educated members of rural communities towards urban areas. It is not unusual to find migrants into an area having average levels of education higher than those in the population they join.

TABLE 3.6 Educational attainment index* by income group

Income level	Tugurio neighbourhoods		Other neighbourhoods		Total San José	
	Migrant	Non-migrant	Migrant	Non-migrant	Migrant	Non-migrant
All income groups	0.49	0.24	0.63	0.21	0.60	0.21
Higher than ₡2000 ($260)	0.53	0.22	0.68	0.19	0.66	0.20
Less than ₡2000	0.45	0.27	0.52	0.25	0.51	0.25
Less than ₡1300 ($170)	0.43	0.30	0.53	0.29	0.51	0.29

NOTES
Colones converted at 7.7 per US $1.00.
*The index is defined as the number of completed years of schooling divided by 11, the number of years in the Costa Rican primary and secondary educational system.

SOURCE
See Table 3.1.

TABLE 3.7 Unemployment rate (percentage) by income group

Income level	Tugurio neighbourhoods		Other neighbourhoods		Total San José	
	Migrant	Non-migrant	Migrant	Non-migrant	Migrant	Non-migrant
All income groups	8	8	5	6	6	5
Higher than ₡2000 ($260)	3	4	2	3	2	3
Less than ₡2000	16	15	14	14	15	14
Less than ₡1300 ($170)	21	21	22	21	22	21

NOTE
Colones converted at 7.7 per US $1.00.

SOURCE
See Table 3.1.

Nevertheless, the superior education of migrants indicated by the Costa Rican data is far beyond normal expectations, and additional research would be needed to validate these findings.

Unemployment rates

Poor people have higher unemployment rates than richer ones. In general, however, poor people in *tugurios* did not have higher unemployment rates than poor people who lived in more comfortable neighbourhoods, nor do migrants appear to be uniquely disadvantaged in the *tugurios*. Their unemployment rates in these deteriorated zones were nearly equal to those of non-migrants, as Table 3.7 indicates. Once again, the popular impressions of the severe and special disadvantages under which the migrants were working are simply contradicted by these census tabulations.

Conclusions from census tabulations

While the census tabulations may contradict some conventional wisdom about where migrants lived, what they earned, and how unemployed they were, these findings are not at variance with studies of urban migration to other Latin American capitals.[4] How can the difference between popular impression and survey results be explained? The general consciousness of the growth of slums and shantytowns in newly urbanised zones is widespread, in no small part because of their physical ugliness. The notion of more urban migrants themselves is also common. But connecting the two confuses correlation and causation.

The increase in numbers of urban migrants in San José correlated with many other phenomena occurring over time: growth of the urban centre, of cinemas and fast-food outlets, of diesel taxicabs, and so forth. Few observers would connect migration to these other, time-related phenomena. As shown by the census results, it seems equally fallacious to assign to migration the leading role in explaining the growth of *tugurio* districts.

MIGRATION'S IMPACT

Our observations show that migration, while clearly a force in the process of urban growth of the San José Metropolitan Area, was not its primary generator. Rather, it accounted for only one-third of the city's total population growth in the intercensal period ending in 1973. The rate of migration did not accelerate. Nor were the migrants, whatever their level of poverty and living conditions, considerably more disadvantaged than the non-migrant population of the city.

Naturally, one must treat these findings with great care. No one suggests that the migrants 'had it easy', or that they lived under conditions that, on the whole, might be labelled satisfactory. Policy responses to the problems of poverty can obviously help migrants at the same time they help the poor in general.

Nevertheless, the foregoing analysis seems to suggest that special policies oriented towards easing the specific problems of the migrant population were not of first priority, given the equivalent incidence of poverty among other poor in San José. As described further in chapter 8, the National Planning Office (OFIPLAN) included in its five-year plan some policy statements advocating national economic integration and decentralisation.[5] Such policies are standard fare in Latin American countries faced by the problems associated with the existence of a large capital city relative to other national urban centres and with regional income differentials of a magnitude sufficient to generate urban migration. While such policies in Costa Rica were sensible, our findings show that they are not warranted as a specific response to overwhelming problems of migrants.

APPENDIX

INTERNAL MIGRATION AND THE URBAN AGGLOMERATION

Because it is geographically more compact and because the 1977 Household and Adult Surveys were limited to it, the unit of analysis treated in chapter 3 is the San José Metropolitan Area. If the larger Urban Agglomeration were treated, the conclusions about the speed and impact of migration would be altered. Therefore, for future studies, inclusion of the cities of Alajuela, Heredia, and Cartago and their immediate hinterlands in the unit of analysis would be advisable.

One estimate of the rates of natural increase and of migration for the larger Agglomeration is as follows:[6]

Rates (per thousand)	1950–63	1963–73
Birth rate	44	34
Death rate	8.5	6
Rate of natural increase	35.5	28
Rate of net immigration	5	10
Rate of population increase	40.5	38

Clearly this estimate shows an acceleration not only in the numbers of net immigrants, but in the rate of their immigration – an acceleration not manifested in any data available for the smaller Metropolitan Area. It indicates that these areas in the belt around the Metropolitan Area were the recipients of current migratory streams. It should be noted that persons residing in this circumferential belt were not included in our analysis, and therefore that our conclusions are based only on the smaller Metropolitan Area as defined on page 10.

4 Employment

INTRODUCTION

Poverty is related in part to jobs and earnings. Not all poverty, however, can be explained this way, as the chapter on poverty has noted. But the appeal of putting unemployed people to work, of increasing the incomes of some poor people, and of transmitting the sense of dignity and human worth associated with regular employment motivates a careful inspection of employment and its relation to poverty.

This chapter reviews employment between 1963 and 1976 for Costa Rica as a whole and for the San José Metropolitan Area. It looks in more detail at employment conditions in the neighbourhoods most closely identified with physical deterioration (*tugurios*). It inquires into the possibilities and problems associated with *tugurio*-specific employment policies. It discusses generalised labour market conditions and their implications for labour force projections. It considers policies for employment generation that flow from two industrial surveys. Finally, it explores policy alternatives in general that link employment and poverty. A set of twenty tables providing considerable detail is appended to the chapter and is cited throughout.

EVOLUTION OF EMPLOYMENT IN COSTA RICA, 1963–76

Economy-wide changes in employment

Local labour markets and individual welfare are closely associated with economy-wide changes in employment. A comparison of employment growth shows a somewhat larger increase during the period 1973–6 than in the earlier intercensal years 1963–73. The annual average of additional employment rose from about 17,500 new jobs to about 24,000 new jobs per year between the two periods (see table 4.A.1; the 'A' in the table's number indicates its

47

location in the appendix to this chapter). The increase has been interpreted as especially encouraging, since annual growth of national product during the latter period was less than it had been earlier (Table 4.A.2).

Sectoral changes in employment

Economy-wide changes are transmitted to different economic activities at different rates. Sectoral differentials in income elasticity of demand, on one side, and differential changes in productivity, on the other, lead to different rates of growth of sectoral employment within the economy.[1] The Costa Rican manifestations of these changes are representative of the process in many developing nations. We see the gradual decline of agriculture as an employer, an increase in absolute and relative terms of non-agricultural employment, and the rapid growth of public employment as compared with private economic activities.

The agricultural sector has traditionally been not only the 'motor' sector of the national economy but also the greatest source of employment. But economic development after about 1960 in Costa Rica has been based largely on the establishment of the Central American Common Market and on the accompanying growth of industrial and other non-agricultural activities.

From 1963 to 1976 agriculture's share of employment fell from 49.7 per cent to 34.8 per cent, while in terms of output its relative importance remained nearly constant (Tables 4.A.1 and 4.A.2). This reflected increased productivity by agricultural workers caused essentially by the greater use of fertilisers, mechanisation, and irrigation, as well as changes in the composition of output. The change in composition of agricultural output, towards livestock raising, for example, had its negative effects on the demand for labour, given the low intensity of labour use in livestock raising. The diminution in requirements for labour in the countryside based on these technological advances, and a greater need for workers in industrial, commercial and service activities, produced a structural transformation. While agricultural employment grew in the period 1963 to 1973 at an average annual rate of 1.3 per cent, non-agricultural employment grew at rates higher than 5 per cent, with employment in the commerce sector growing even faster, at a rate of 8.2 per cent.

Favourable changes in the employment situation following 1973 are primarily attributable to the satisfactory absorptive capacity of the industrial, commerce, and governmental sectors, in which employment rose at rates of 8.8, 8.0, and 6.1 per cent, respectively. This employment growth was accompanied by a decline in worker productivity. A calculation of industrial labour productivity shows a decline from 19,600 Costa Rican colones in 1973 to 18,600 in 1976.[2] The fall in productivity could signify that the increase in employment levels was due to underutilisation of the industrial labour force. Alternatively, the increased employment levels could have been a result of more labour-intensive techniques in the industrial process.

The relatively rapid growth of the industrial sector, aided enormously by the process of Central American economic integration, exercised a strong magnetism over rural workers who were attracted by the higher incomes and better conditions of city life. This process led to substantial rural–urban migration and, consequently, to a relatively high rate of growth in the urban labour force (5.7 per cent against 2.8 per cent in the rural sector from 1963 to 1976). If the industrial sector had not been so dynamic, unemployment rates would have been considerably higher. As an illustration, after 1973, the urban labour force did grow slightly faster than employment. However, during this period, employment in the industrial sector grew at a much higher rate (8.8 per cent). The rate of growth in employment in the construction and service sectors was much lower, resulting in the 5.5 per cent average. These figures are presented in greater detail in Tables 4.A.3 and 4.A.4.

Expansion in the public sector also helped to keep employment abreast of growth in the labour force. Various economists have suggested that the public sector may act as an employer of last resort, that is, as the absorber of residual labour. In 1950 only 6.2 per cent of total employment was found in the public sector. By 1976 the figure had grown to 16.6 per cent. It should be emphasised that within the public sector, autonomous state enterprises increased their participation from 1.0 per cent in 1950 to 8.6 per cent of total employment in 1973. The rate of growth of autonomous institution employment slowed down after 1973, resulting in an 8.8 per cent share of total employment in 1976 (Table 4.A.9).

Regional changes in employment

Aggregate movements and their sectoral outcomes have spatial repercussions as well. One might apply the same conceptual framework, relying on urban–rural differentials in income elasticities of demand and in productivity change. The results underlie the familiar process of urbanisation, seen in Costa Rica as readily as in other low-income countries.

Urban employment in Costa Rica grew faster than rural employment, a phenomenon clearly related to structural changes in the economy. Rural employment did increase slightly in absolute terms from 1973 to 1976, although at a lower rate than the rural labour force. There was a simultaneous drop in rural unemployment and increased rate of growth of urban unemployment (Table 4.A.4). As rural emigrants left, they reduced employment pressures in the rural areas. At the same time, labour supply pressures increased in the modern urban sector.

Thus, greater concentration of the national labour force in urban areas occurred (Table 4.A.3). The urban labour force and urban employment rose at twice the annual rates of the rural areas. Even though urban employment increased at a slightly lower rate than the labour force, serious unemployment problems were avoided because of the labour absorption capabilities of the industry, commerce, service, and public sectors.

During the 1970s, the cities of Costa Rica showed a remarkable capacity to absorb new workers. Should this change, the face of poverty would change dramatically. The rate of population growth fell in both urban and rural areas over the 1973–76 period, but during this time, urban population growth rates were five times higher than rural rates (Table 4.A.4). The development of new urban jobs nevertheless kept pace.

Changing roles for women

Opening new employment opportunities for women in the urban economy of Costa Rica had major implications for poverty on several counts. First, it represented the incorporation of a vast pool of previously untapped human resources into the labour market. Second, the income earned by women created new domestic markets for Costa Rican goods and services. Third, it affected the continuing decline of birth rates, by providing women with visible alternatives to child-rearing, by instilling a stronger sense of economic security, and by reinforcing preferences for smaller families. Easy explanations exist for the rise in women's labour force participation. The agricultural sector, with its relative lack of female employment opportunities, became less important. Modern sector jobs, whose numbers grew rapidly, required less physical strength as mechanisation progressed. Educational attainment among women rose, increasing their desirability as employees. Social attitudes grew more tolerant of women working outside the home for pay. And the declining birth rate itself liberated women from some of the burdens of child care, allowing them to go into the labour market.

UNEMPLOYMENT

Interest in unemployment in general stems from at least three sources. Unemployment represents unused economic resources: in this case, unused inputs of labour. Unless labour's marginal product is zero, lower measured rates of unemployment would normally accompany higher output for the economy as a whole. Unemployment also implies economic deprivation from lower incomes. Unemployment compensation and other income transfers, even when available, only partially offset the income losses that usually accompany unemployment. Finally, in most cultures productive employment lends social status, and the state of unemployment is correspondingly associated with a lower sense of dignity or self-worth.[3]

Measuring open unemployment in poor countries faces challenges even greater than the difficulties present elsewhere. It is hard in many individual cases to differentiate satisfactorily between being 'unemployed' and 'out of the labour force'. Since relatively more workers are self-employed, the question, 'Did you work last week?' is answered affirmatively, although the economic value of the output, to the economy and to the worker, may be very low indeed. The greater prevalence of irregular or casual employment implies the presence of a larger degree of randomness in even the most candid responses than would be experienced in affluent countries. And the problems of measuring open unemployment in rural areas, even when these regions contain the bulk of a country's population, are well known.

As noted earlier, pressures on the Costa Rican labour market in the period 1963–73 did not have a large negative impact on the employment situation, since new employment opportunities were created at an average annual rate exceeding 5 per cent (Table 4.A.2).

The rate of open, measured unemployment fell from 6.9 per cent in 1963 to 6.2 per cent in 1976 (Table 4.A.11). This constituted a drop in both rural and urban unemployment rates: the rural from 6.2 per cent (1963) to 5.8 per cent (1976) and the urban from 8.2 per cent to 6.8 per cent (Table 4.A.12). At all times, urban unemployment rates exceeded rural rates, for reasons associated with the structure of employment in both places. In particular, self-employment is more prevalent in the countryside than in the city, and therefore the possibilities for open, measured unemployment are accordingly lower.

In the period 1973–76, the numbers of persons unemployed in cities grew at an average annual rate of 7.2 per cent, while rural unemployment dropped at a rate of 8.4 per cent (Table 4.A.4). We note as well that during the earlier period, 1963–73, the rate of growth of rural unemployment was higher than that in cities, but owing to rural–urban migration, the relation was reversed after 1973 (Table 4.A.4).

Female unemployment rose notably, primarily among women below nineteen years of age (Table 4.A.11). While female unemployment rates rose in all age groups, male rates fell during the period 1963–76. This was accompanied by reduced participation rates for men of all ages, and increased participation rates for all but the oldest women.

Underemployment

Underemployment is measured in two ways in Costa Rica. 'Visible' underemployment measures the desire of workers to work longer hours – a desire that has not been fulfilled owing to 'lack of work'. The number of equivalent jobs required to eliminate visible underemployment in 1976 amounted to 2.8 per cent of the total labour force (Tables 4.A.13 and 4.A.20). By definition, persons who received less than ₡600 per month in 1976 and who worked more than forty-seven hours weekly were classified as invisibly underemployed. The number of additional jobs to employ them fully amounted to the equivalent of 4.1 per cent of the workforce.

EMPLOYMENT IN SAN JOSÉ

While national economic trends affect all areas of the country, our particular interest in this work centres on the San José Metropolitan Area. Its concentration of population, workforce, industrial activity, cultural affairs, and governmental offices is typical of the urban situation in many other developing countries.

In July 1976 the Metropolitan Area of San José had about 550,000 inhabitants or 27.3 per cent of the total population of the country (Table 4.A.14). Between 1963 and 1973, the average rate of population growth in San José was 4.4 per cent per year, while in the period 1973–76, it was 3.5 per cent. Both rates are higher than the average annual rates for the country as a whole for the same periods (3.4 and 2.3 per cent, respectively).

The rate of participation, unadjusted for age composition differences, was the highest in the country: 35.7 per cent (Tables 4.A.12, 4.A.14, and 4.A.15). It is interesting to note that labour force participation rates of migrants to the San José Metropolitan Area were also high (Table 4.A.16). This suggests that the Metropolitan Area rate might have been high because of the growing number of migrants. But, perhaps more importantly, the high participation rates of migrants indicate that increased rural–urban migration would have an even stronger impact on the supply side of the labour market.

Available workers in San José were absorbed largely in the non-agricultural sectors (manufacturing, services, and commerce) which jointly contributed 83.3 per cent of total employment in 1976 and 81.7 per cent in 1973 (Table 4.A.19).

In 1976, the unemployment rate in San José was 6.1 per cent. In the country as a whole, it was 6.2 per cent, while in all urban areas it was 6.8 per cent. The lower rate of unemployment in San José may have reflected the modern sector's greater need for workers, especially given its dynamic growth. Nevertheless, it is not clear to what extent the capacity for labour absorption was greater in the modern sector than in traditional activities. Seasonal influences are relevant in this matter, since rural employment, which by its nature undergoes seasonal fluctuations, is relatively low in the month of July. We note parenthetically, however, that the three surveys on which our conclusions are based were done in May (1973 census), July (1976 employment survey), and May–June (1977 *tugurio* survey).

Turning from unemployment to underemployment, the amounts

of underemployment have been translated into equivalent unemployment rates in Table 4.A.20. For San José, underemployment was less than that experienced outside the capital, whether in other cities, in rural zones, or in the rest of the country as a whole. Nevertheless, the underutilisation of labour in San José represented a high cost for the national economy. The capital's situation found 8 per cent of the labour force underemployed. We conclude that economic policy objectives ought not to concentrate on combating open unemployment alone, but ought as well to seek higher productivity, more jobs, and greater opportunities for workers who are employed but underutilised.

NOMINAL WAGES AND REAL WAGES

Minimum wages of the lowest paid occupations are one indicator of incomes of the poor and near poor. Costa Rican minimum wages, like those of some other Latin American countries, are highly specific to different occupations within each branch of economic activity. For example, to outline the minimum wages in manufacturing, fourteen tightly spaced pages were used in classifying different industries and occupations in the Ministry of Labour's instructional guide for 1977. The highest minimum wages were assigned to chemical analysts and newspaper proofreaders, while the lowest went to unskilled workers in a variety of industries. The highest specified minimum wages were 2.6 times higher than the lowest.

The mid-1970s were marked by what appears to have been a transitory spurt of inflation in Costa Rica. During this period, however, minimum wages rose faster than living costs as measured by the consumer price index. While prices increased by some 60 per cent between 1973 and 1977, official minimum wages rose by an even larger factor. The result was an increase in purchasing power in current prices from 14 to 33 per cent over the four-year period, at least for people holding jobs governed by minimum wages. Looking instead at salaries for workers covered by Social Security (some 70 per cent of the labour force as of 1976), it is less apparent that wages kept pace with inflation. These average salaries are shown in Table 4.1. It should also be noted that these average salaries were probably overvalued since those not covered by Social Security are likely to receive lower wages.

TABLE 4.1 Indices of prices, nominal salaries and real salaries

Year	Consumer price index	Salaries							
		Agriculture		Industry		Other		Total	
		Nominal	Real	Nominal	Real	Nominal	Real	Nominal	Real
1972	1.00	1.00	1.00	1.00	1.00	1.00	1.00	1.00	1.00
1973	1.127	1.148	1.019	1.089	0.966	1.070	0.949	1.094	0.971
1974	1.499	1.321	0.881	1.292	0.862	1.243	0.829	1.280	0.854
1975	1.760	1.627	0.924	1.534	0.872	1.495	0.849	1.546	0.878
1976	1.822	1.906	1.046	1.822	1.000	1.737	0.953	1.815	0.996

THE *TUGURIO* EMPLOYMENT SITUATION

Throughout our study of poverty in Costa Rica, we have been centrally concerned with its spatial location both in its direct manifestations and underlying causes. A natural target of concern is unemployment in *tugurios*. Idle slum workers are a stereotypical image of poverty. The natural response proposes employment-generation projects in poor neighbourhoods.

We have no specific quarrel with such policies, but data from Costa Rica make it clear that slum-focused solutions by themselves are an over-simplified and highly biased view of the poverty problem. The evidence suggests that the severity of unemployment in *tugurios* was not very different from the same problem encountered in other parts of the city or the country. In this sense, identifying poverty as uniquely or even principally a *slum* phenomenon is clearly incorrect, both as an approach to understanding its causes and as a guide to formulating effective policy. The danger lies in the implicit assumption that if the problem of slums were solved, the problem of poverty would be simultaneously eradicated. The data strongly suggest otherwise.

Background

In 1973, the San José Metropolitan Area had about half a million residents, grouped in nearly 100,000 families. Of these, 75,000 people, or about 15 per cent of the population, lived in areas designed by the Costa Rican National Housing Agency, INVU, as 'deteriorated zones' or '*tugurios*' (Table 4.2). These zones

TABLE 4.2   1973 population in *tugurios* and non-*tugurios*, San José Metropolitan Area, in thousands

Metropolitan Area, total:	
Population	501
No. of families	94
Of which, *tugurios*:	
Population	73
Families	13
And non-*tugurios*:	
Population	428
Families	83

constituted the city's neighbourhoods of slums, shacks, and shantytowns.

In the years between 1973 and 1976 the Metropolitan Area population grew through migration and natural increase at a rate estimated by the Ministry of Labour to be 3.2 per cent per year. No independent data exist on the separate rates of growth of *tugurios* and other urban areas.

Unemployment rates

Open, measured unemployment as a proportion of the labour force was higher in the *tugurios* than elsewhere. While these measurements are surrounded by problems involving the census and survey processes, the rates appear to have risen between 1973, when the census tabulated *tugurio* unemployment at about 8 per cent, and 1977 when a household survey in the same areas registered a 9.9 per cent rate. Also, it should be noted that *tugurio* unemployment seems to have increased during the same period in which unemployment in the entire Metropolitan Area fell. Some details are recited in Table 4.3.

The age–sex composition of unemployment allows further insights into the problems of joblessness. As shown in Table 4.4, both male and female unemployment rates in *tugurios* were higher than those outside. The most notable differential was associated with *tugurio* males over forty-five years of age, whose unemployment rates (15.3 per cent) were more than six times the rates for this cohort in San José taken as a whole. Even female unemployment rates in the same age group were more than double those of the urban zone.

TABLE 4.3 Unemployment in *tugurios* and elsewhere

Unemployment rate in *tugurios:*	
1973 census	8.0%
1977 household survey	9.9%
Unemployment outside *tugurios* in the San José Metropolitan Area:	
1973 census	5.0%
Unemployment in the San José Metropolitan Area as a whole:	
1973 census	6.6%
1976 employment survey	6.1%

TABLE 4.4 San José: age composition, labour force participation rates, and open unemployment rates, by age and sex, according to *tugurio* residence (1977) and Metropolitan Area as a whole (1976) (all figures are percentages)

Sex	Age	Age composition		Labour force participation rate		Unemployment rate	
		Metro. Area 1976 %	Tugurios 1977 %	Metro. Area 1976 %	Tugurios 1977 %	Metro. Area 1976 %	Tugurios 1977 %
Both sexes	Total	100.0	100.0	35.7	36.7	6.0	9.9
	Less than 12	28.1	31.4	–	–	–	–
	12–19	20.0	21.5	28.5	37.0	16.8	15.3
	20–44	33.7	33.0	65.5	67.6	4.6	6.9
	45–64	13.3	10.1	52.4	54.2	2.4	13.1
	65 and over	4.8	3.6	19.9	26.2	–	–
	not known	0.1	0.4	66.7	50.0	–	–
Men	Total	100.0	100.0	49.7	54.0	6.1	10.5
	Less than 12	29.9	32.2	–	–	–	–
	12–19	21.3	21.5	34.6	50.0	19.8	17.0
	20–44	31.8	34.1	91.7	97.2	4.4	7.1
	45–64	13.0	8.6	87.9	94.5	2.3	15.3
	65 and over	3.9	3.4	43.7	48.0	–	–
	not known	0.1	0.3	66.7	100.0	–	–
Women	Total	100.0	100.0	22.9	19.9	6.0	8.1
	Less than 12	26.6	30.7	–	–	–	–
	12–19	18.8	21.4	22.1	24.1	11.9	11.7
	20–44	35.4	31.9	44.0	36.1	5.1	6.4
	45–64	13.5	11.7	21.1	24.7	3.0	6.4
	65 and over	5.6	3.8	4.8	7.0	–	–
	not known	0.1	0.5	66.7	14.3	–	–

SOURCES
1976. *Encuesta nacional de hogares—empleo y desempleo—julio 1976*, table 6.
1977. Tabulations from *tugurio* survey done by the Oficina de Información. (Household survey, *not* the adult survey.) See the Appendix for details.

Policy measures regarding employment can clearly focus on this group and on their special characteristics. These people were unemployed rather than 'inactive', that is, they actively sought work as part of the labour force, and the vast majority were from forty-five to sixty-four years of age (Table 4.4).

While overall unemployment rates, and rates by age–sex cohorts, were higher in the *tugurios* than elsewhere in San José, the same cannot be said when the data are standardised by income levels (Table 4.5). Among persons living in families with low incomes, unemployment rates in *tugurios* and non-*tugurios* were nearly equal. Not surprisingly, persons in low-income families had unemployment rates considerably above the area-wide averages. As Table 4.5 shows, about a quarter of the lowest income males qualified as openly unemployed, no matter where they lived. This was the obvious target group for employment policy.

TABLE 4.5 Unemployment rates in *tugurios* and elsewhere, by sex and income group

1973 Income per capita	Tugurios		Non-tugurios	
	Labour force size	*Unemploy- ment rate*	*Labour force size*	*Unemploy- ment rate*
All incomes:				
Men	17200	9%	94300	6%
Women	5900	5	47600	2
Less than ₡1300 ($170)				
Men	3300	24	9300	25
Women	1100	11	3400	9
Less than ₡2000 ($260)				
Men	6900	17	21600	16
Women	2200	9	7500	7

EMPLOYMENT POTENTIAL WITHIN *TUGURIOS*

Comparisons cited above between *tugurio* and non-*tugurio* conditions are based mainly on 1973 census data. A closer look at employment prospects within *tugurios* themselves can be gained from the results of a 1977 survey of 517 household heads in a sample of *tugurios* within the San José Metropolitan Area. An appendix at the end of this chapter describes this data source.

A one-time-only survey of this kind is a useful complement to periodic census data, dealing with the question of poverty on a more highly focused level. This particular survey was designed to focus on the poor. It contemplated specific forms of policy follow up, along the lines of housing and employment-generation projects. The results are not very useful for comparing *tugurios* with non-*tugurios*, because the questions asked about poverty were specifically composed to deal with the particular conditions known to exist in *tugurios*. Measures of unemployment, for example, were not the same as those used by the national census, yielding different estimates. These estimates were neither better nor worse than census estimates; they simply looked at different facets of what it means to be employed or unemployed, 'capable' of working or not, and 'actively' seeking jobs or not. This is consistent with our general point about understanding poverty: it is a process that must be traced through a variety of geographic levels, using a variety of methods: some are needed for an up close, first-hand look at the human face of poverty, others for standing back to see larger forces at work; some for seeing its special characteristics in territorial pockets, some for tracking down the ways it is woven into the larger fabric of social processes.

TUGURIO SURVEY FINDINGS

Of the 517 adults surveyed, 56 per cent had worked during the previous week, while the remainder had not. Of those not working, the largest number (61 per cent) were housewives, followed by those out of work (14 per cent), students (11 per cent) and others (14 per cent).

Definitions of open unemployment vary, according to the use to which the measurements will be put. The periodic Employment Surveys of the Ministry of Labour count as 'unemployed' those persons who did not work during the survey week and who, at the same time, actively sought work. The construction of the *tugurio* survey questionnaire does not permit reliable comparison with the Employment Surveys and the 1973 and 1976 data cited earlier.

The survey considered housewives to be the only economically inactive group that was potentially active. Accordingly, they were asked about their possible participation in order to determine the possibility of adding to a family's money income by adding an extra income earner to the workforce.

Nearly 63 per cent of all housewives (one-sixth of all adults) said they would like to work, although the vast majority wanted only part-time work.[4] Such a finding is consonant with child-care and housekeeping responsibilities in a culture in which males seldom undertaken either. It is also similar to observations of new female labour force participation in more affluent countries, in which the women actively pursue part-time work as a transition between full-time housekeeping duties and a full-time job. The survey did not determine whether any of these women had taken concrete steps to seek work.

As mentioned above, more than half the adults were gainfully occupied, and nearly a quarter more had been employed formerly. There are no data on the age and sex composition of this latter group, but it is possible to speculate that it consists largely of the openly unemployed and of housewives and students who, at one time, held jobs. Of the group formerly employed, more than half (58 per cent) had not held a job in the last two years, indicating a reasonably lengthy separation from active labour force participation. The remaining 19 per cent of the sample had never been employed.

The survey questionnaire also tried to determine the present means of support for the formerly employed. Marriage was the most prevalent, followed by intra-family transfer payments. No member of the sample received transfer payments in cash from the government, according to the survey's responses.

Urban development theoreticians often assert that workers in a slum form a vast and largely unstructured pool, in which employment is transitory and self-employment common. However, in San José's *tugurios*, only about one-sixth of the respondents were (or had been) temporary employees, self-employed, or other.[5] This is due primarily to the attractiveness of more favourable wages and working conditions for 'employees', coupled with the satisfactory growth of demand for workers in San José during the recent past.

The bulk of the workforce was in urban tertiary activities, including the services (44 per cent), followed by 33 per cent in secondary activities, and 4 per cent in primary activities.

A substantial portion of all these jobs are in very small firms. About 30 per cent of the adults sampled worked in firms with fewer than ten employees, and 45 per cent worked in firms with more than ten. Very few workers had exercised managerial responsibilities – only 7 per cent against 74 per cent who had not.

Employment instability was, at least on first impression,

surprisingly high. Of the respondents, one-fifth had less than a single year in their present jobs. Many explanations can be offered. First, physical and mental infirmity may prevent some *tugurio* residents from holding down jobs for long periods of time. Second, turnover among young people, who are disproportionately found in these neighbourhoods, is higher than among older people. Third, problems with transport may contribute to turnover. Unfortunately, the survey data do not permit us to choose among these alternative hypotheses. However, there are some benefits from high turnover, especially for young people: they gain experience in a variety of jobs before determining the type of work they will eventually choose.

Multiple job holding might be thought to be characteristic of persons living in poverty. The survey, however, showed very little:

Single job holders	55%	
Multiple job holders	1%	
Sub-total	56%	of sample

The survey of *tugurio* adults sought detailed information about the multiple sources of income that sometimes are observed in situations in which self-employment and cottage industry may be important elements in overall family income. The results were as follows (figures are percentages):

Wages in cash	56%
Wages in kind	5
Profits from sale of:	
Cooked food	1
Garden output	1
Artisan products	0
Purchased goods	2
Rent of houses	2
of rooms	1
Imputed rents (for home owners)	39

These data show that the majority of income earners were salaried. The unexpectedly high attachment of the workforce to employer–employee relationships is not easy to interpret. One plausible interpretation is that the *tugurios* are better incorporated into the urban economy and into its formal labour markets than might have been assumed.[6]

The survey noted that 39 per cent of the respondents could be credited with earning imputed rents. Homeowners, therefore, have higher disposable income, other things being equal, than persons who must pay rent. Unfortunately other sources of imputed income were not determined (for example, value of home-grown fruits and vegetables, or home-made products by artisans), although we can say that the value of these would be less than imputed rents.

Workers were asked in the survey whether they felt a lack of adequate training. About a quarter of those who had worked the previous week said they were working in jobs for which their backgrounds were not completely adequate.[7] This seems to indicate that there could be a greater emphasis on vocational education or subsidised on-the-job training of one kind or another.

Workers may, at the same time, be more broadly trained than is indicated by the particular job they happen to be holding at the time of the survey. While responses must be viewed with appropriate scepticism, it is useful to note that only 9 per cent of all the adults surveyed admitted that they were capable of only a single trade or occupation.

Nineteen per cent of the respondents were attending training courses of one kind or another. Of the total sample, 6 per cent were at the National Apprenticeship Institute; 4 per cent in commercial schools; 2 per cent in sewing courses; and 7 per cent in other. An even greater proportion responded positively to a question about their willingness to attend a course (or to attend another course, as the case may be) – 68 per cent said they would attend a course, while only 28 per cent said they would not.

A number of findings from the *tugurio* survey seem to have direct implications for design of policy interventions. We will return to these in a later chapter, but a brief summary is appropriate here.

Tugurio family heads tend to be young. Many of the workforce members are inexperienced and undertrained, and a large proportion are desirous of or amenable to some form of additional job training. There seems to be both the need and the opportunity for skill upgrading, assuming opportunity and access to related employment and promotion.

About 10 per cent of the *tugurio* workers received their wages in kind or from sale of food and artisan products – suggestive of 'informal' sector employment, and probably very low wages. A much larger proportion of the workers was employed by very small businesses with less than ten employees. The small scale sector in particular offers an important source of employment for *tugurio* residents. Expanded opportunities in this sector should be explored.

Finally, there was a considerable break in time since last employment for those who were unemployed, suggesting a considerable lack of mobility in employment conditions for a sizeable number of *tugurio* residents.

MARKET MECHANISM FAILURES: HOW MUCH CONTRIBUTION TO UNEMPLOYMENT?

In a free-market or mixed economy, one of the chief explanations of poverty often put forward is the failure of market structures. In the case of Costa Rica, and in the more general context of 'lesser developed regions', we are not talking about business cycles or major crises such as the Great Depression. The question is whether market mechanisms are generally doing an effective job of equilibrating supply and demand. In the case of employment, we are specifically concerned with the supply and demand for labour, and the ability of the market to adjust for anticipated changes in supply or demand for jobs.

Much economic and social planning, especially in poor countries, revolves around the implicit assumption that market mechanisms do not function effectively in achieving this equilibrium. Projection techniques are employed to estimate future gaps, and specific policies designed to close the gaps. This kind of planning effort assumes that the market itself cannot cope with the gaps as they arise.

Of course the smooth operation of markets does not necessarily imply a utopian situation. It does mean that policy intervention based on the size of the overall gap between labour supply and demand is likely to be excessively simplistic and notably inefficient when markets work reasonably satisfactorily.

Labour market failure as a concept

Possible or potential failure in labour markets would be preceded by early warning signs. These could include:

(a) Rigorous enforcement of legal *minimum wages* at levels inconsistent with worker productivity.
(b) Persistent open *unemployment* of more than, say, 10 per cent of the workforce, especially when existing side-by-side with unfilled vacancies.
(c) Simultaneous presence of wide regional *wage differentials* together with absence of internal migration from low to high wage areas.
(d) Massive social and political *discontent* focused on unsatisfactory present institutional responses to public pressures.

Labour markets in San José

In a mixed economy when the signs noted above are absent, one would conclude that labour markets were, in fact, working. In Costa Rica, and particularly in San José, markets displayed characteristics suggestive of adjustment rather than failure.

(a) A system of legal *minimum wages*, promulgated by the Ministry of Labour, which was adjusted annually and differentiated by occupation. Urban self-employment existed as a safety valve to these minima. Of those employed for wages, about one-tenth of the full-time workers earned, on the average, less than two-thirds of the minimum wage, thereby reflecting their productivity.
(b) Open, measured *unemployment* in 1973 of 6.6 per cent and in July 1976 of 6.1 per cent. These figures were similar to those observed in affluent industrialised countries and were considerably less than the 10 or even 15 per cent rates seen in some low-income countries.
(c) Regional *wage differentials* stimulated urban migration at rates comparable to those in other developing countries.
(d) Absence of massive *discontent*. Uncontrollable demonstrations, riots, sabotage, kidnapping, and other forms of violence, while notable in some other countries, were absent in Costa Rica. At the same time, the republic had free elections and a free press.

These characteristics suggest that labour markets in San José worked relatively well. Their presence calls into question any recommendations based on the alleged presence of 'structural disequilibria', that is, of (labour) market failure.

The Short Term Future

Markets, working relatively smoothly at a given date, could be strained beyond their limits under a number of possible conditions: labour force expansion of unprecedented speed; fall in the rate of growth of industrial and other modern urban sectors; and/or change in the composition of demand for labour, especially towards scarce skills and away from skills possessed by the bulk of the existing labour force. Each of these possibilities should be assessed in determining ultimately the labour market policies appropriate for urban poverty.

With regard to each of these factors, we foresaw the following for San José:

(a) Growth of the labour force

The labour force in San José during the mid-1970s grew at approximately 4.2 per cent per annum, compared with a national average of 4.0 per cent. Population projections for the Metropolitan Area did not foresee an acceleration of population growth in the working ages, so the labour force should not increase greatly and should not create serious difficulties.

Of course, labour force participation rates could change, especially if the participation of women continued to increase. This has been offset, however, by a diminution in the participation of the young of both sexes, who stay in school longer, and the old, a greater number of whom leave the urban labour force to retire on pensions. Those forces seemed likely to continue, leaving overall labour force participation rates largely constant. Hence, with falling rates of natural population growth, and assuming no great increase in rural–urban migration, and constant labour force participation rates, the rates of labour force growth may well decline rather than accelerate.

In summary, we feel that labour market mechanisms would not be strained by unprecedented speed in labour force growth rates in San José.

(b) Growth in overall demand for labour

If growth in Costa Rican output were threatened in the future, rates of expansion of the urban labour force could suffer. No obvious international or domestic barriers to further economic

growth were foreseen, however, and it was assumed that there
would be sufficient stimulus to growth. In addition, employment in
San José was partially insulated from economic fluctuations in the
short run because of the large role of public sector activities.

(c) Composition of demand for labour

The capital intensity of production undoubtedly would continue to
increase as an inevitable concomitant to development. The demand
for specialised workers, embodying large amounts of human
capital, could be expected to grow as well, since physical and
human capital are complementary inputs to the production process.
However, there were no indications of drastic change in the
near-term demand for labour. We cannot foresee large-scale
unfillable vacancies or large groups of skilled workers whose skills
have been made obsolete overnight.

The problems of poverty are by no means limited to problems of
unemployment. Nevertheless, with the preceding analysis of
employment fresh in mind, certain policy conclusions are worth
considering in the closing section of this chapter.

EMPLOYMENT POLICY IMPLICATIONS

Although labour markets in San José worked relatively well and
there appeared to be no need for macro supply and demand
projections, a number of employment policy recommendations can
be made. More detailed recommendations would require additional
surveys of vacancies and expected vacancies at the establishment
level. Recommendations relating to both demand and supply
factors follow.

1 Labour demand

Demand for labour could be stimulated by a number of policy
measures:

(a) Appropriate policies on factor prices

Labour's wages and labour costs in general ought not to be artifici-
ally propped up (for example, through unrealistic minimum wage

levels) since this clearly discourages the use of labour, especially unskilled labour. Analogously, to the extent that capital investment is subsidised, the price of capital falls relative to labour's wage costs, and greater capital intensity in the production process occurs, with a correspondingly lower demand for labour, other things being equal. Periodic changes in factor prices should not exceed changes in factor productivity, especially with regard to the minimum wage. Implementation of this recommendation would require detailed studies of sectoral labour productivity, as well as the political determination to resist popular but exaggerated increases in the minimum wage.

(b) Emphasis on the use of intermediate technology

Intermediate technology should be used wherever possible, rather than highly sophisticated technology developed in foreign research laboratories to maximise the use of capital and returns on royalties for the licensing of the technology. State funds, together with help from international agencies and private foundations, ought to be allocated for compiling and publicising results found internationally. This is needed since private firms using intermediate technology are likely to be very small, at least at first, and therefore incapable of supporting their own local research laboratories.

(c) Public service employment for the hard-core unskilled unemployed

'Correct' factor prices and the use of intermediate (or 'appropriate') technology will not deal with all unemployment. Rural public works, for example, could benefit society as well as deal with some of the most serious problems of long-term unemployment among unskilled workers. Expansion of public employment, however, is controversial in Costa Rica, given its rapid growth in the recent past. Both budgetary considerations and efficiency may make this recommendation impractical.

(d) Public subsidy of worker-owned firms

The degree of labour intensity of such firms would be a function of the internal competitive demands of the industries considered for such assistance. Technical assistance and credit subsidies could be aimed preferentially at those industries whose rate of growth of employment was highest.

2 Labour supply

The supply of labour could also be influenced by the following measures:

(a) Strengthening the Employment Service

As noted earlier, the public employment service was not an important source of job placements. It could offer, however, some new opportunities to the unemployed in *tugurio* neighbourhoods.

(b) Formal apprenticeship training

The National Apprenticeship Institute is the current headquarters for these activities.

(c) Short training courses

To the extent possible, short courses are superior to longer ones, both because they are less expensive and because they respond more quickly to labour market pressures. Training courses that last for years run the risk that the skills produced will become obsolete too quickly after the course ends, especially when an economy is undergoing dynamic changes.

(d) Subsidised on-the-job training

Like the previous two recommendations, these training courses are aimed at increasing productivity of employable workers. However, in addition to upgrading skills of already employed workers, such training with proper incentives to employers can be applied to new workers drawn from the previously unemployed.

The last three types of training courses mentioned cannot be adequately planned without a detailed survey of labour demand at the establishment level. But with these minor exceptions the other demand and supply policy recommendations do not depend on the existence or size of a projected 'gap' between supply and demand for labour. All would be as appropriate in a full-employment economy as in one featuring high measured unemployment.

The recommendations are desirable also because first, they range over a wide spectrum from very general market stimuli (for example, the factor price recommendations) all the way to very specific and highly focused activities (for example, short training courses); second, the recommendations are independent of one another and may proceed simultaneously or separately; and third, the supply side recommendations are at least potentially capable of being focused on *tugurio* residents, or alternatively on the lowest income groups.

Tugurio-specific employment

With regard to *tugurio*-specific employment problems, it should be remembered that policies to 'help *tugurios*' are really policies to help *tugurio* residents. Residents' income and employment may be aided either by *tugurio*-based employment or by heightening their employability outside *tugurios*. The first is exemplified by the location of employers in *tugurios*; the second by schools, health centres, employment services, and the like. Employment service branches in *tugurios* are likely to be the most direct and, therefore, the most cost effective of the possible programmes. However, the cost to the prospective *tugurio* employers of seeking employees through such formal channels should be assessed prior to a general move in this direction.

BEYOND EMPLOYMENT POLICY

Even the best employment policy cannot cure all poverty. Some people are so 'disadvantaged' that they are beyond the reach of jobs and wage incomes. These are the old, the sick, the mentally and physically handicapped, the abandoned mother with her numerous children – in short, a group of persons for whom training, employment services, apprenticeship, and steady work in general may not be attainable.

How numerous are such people? This group is the hardest to reach by formal surveys, and thus the hardest to measure. One indication comes from the May–June 1977 survey of *tugurios* in San José carried out by the Costa Rican Oficina de Información. In commenting on the interview process, that office noted that almost 5 per cent of the interviews turned out to be *blancos*, that is blank or incomplete. The greater part of these incomplete interviews corresponded to 'personas mentalmente incapacitadas'. No skills of literacy or formal education are necessary to respond to a face-to-face interview. Only minimal mental capacity is needed, given the closed-end nature of the majority of the questions. Yet nearly 5 per cent lacked even this minimal capacity.

Accordingly, the survey's completed interviews did not include this bottom 5 per cent which might be considered the economic basket cases of the *tugurio* neighbourhoods. Note that these were not persons who simply refused to be interviewed. Those made up an additional 2.5 per cent of the total sample size. The *blancos*, instead, were associated with persons who tried to cooperate with the interviewer, but simply found the going too tough.

Incapacity at this level may not be alleviated by standard measures of employment policy. Instead, transfer mechanisms of the modern welfare state may be called for, such as those already in existence through the Costa Rican Institute for Social Assistance (IMAS) and the Family Allowances (Asignaciones Familiares) programmes. In addition, the Government of Costa Rica will need to continue or expand rehabilitation programmes, especially those which can provide productive employment for the disadvantaged.

TABLE 4.A.1 Employment by economic activity, and rates of growth—1963, 1973, and 1976

Type of activity	Numbers of workers			Relative sectoral distribution			Average annual growth rates		
	1963	1973	1976	1963 %	1973 %	1976 %	1963-73 %	1973-76 %	1963-76 %
Total country	368,000	545,000	617,000	100.0	100.0	100.0	4.0	4.2	4.1
Agriculture	183,000	208,000	215,000	49.7	38.2	34.8	1.3	1.0	1.2
Industry[a]	43,000	70,000	90,000	11.7	12.9	14.6	5.0	8.8	5.8
Construction	20,000	38,000	40,000	5.5	6.9	6.5	6.3	2.3	5.4
Basic services[b]	17,000	30,000	34,000	4.8	5.5	5.6	5.5	4.7	5.3
Commerce[c]	36,000	80,000	101,000	9.9	12.2	16.3	8.2	8.0	8.1
Personal services[d]	67,000	119,000	137,000	18.4	24.3	22.1	5.8	4.7	5.6

NOTES
Individual figures have been rounded, and may therefore not sum to column totals shown.
[a]Includes manufacturing and mining.
[b]Includes electricity, gas, water, transportation, communication and storage.
[c]Includes wholesale and retail trade, restaurants, hotels and banking.
[d]Includes the other sectors and activities not well specified.

SOURCE
Adjusted Population Census, 1963 and 1973; and Household Employment Survey, July 1976.

TABLE 4.A.2 Sectoral structure and changes in Gross National Product—1963, 1973 and 1976

Type of activity	GNP^a 1963	GNP^a 1973	GNP^a 1976	Relative sectoral distribution 1963 %	Relative sectoral distribution 1973 %	Relative sectoral distribution 1976 %	Average annual growth rates 1963-73 %	Average annual growth rates 1973-76 %	Average annual growth rates 1963-76 %
Total country	3475	6934	7963	100.0	100.0	100.0	7.1	4.7	6.6
Agriculture	856	1565	1736	24.6	22.6	21.8	6.2	3.5	5.6
Industry^b	591	1373	1681	17.0	19.8	21.1	8.8	7.0	8.4
Construction	195	379	469	5.6	5.5	5.9	6.9	7.3	5.3
Basic services^c	202	504	606	5.8	7.3	7.6	9.6	6.3	8.8
Commerce^d	504	1098	1169	14.5	15.8	14.7	8.1	2.1	6.7
Personal services^e	1128	2014	2303	32.5	29.0	28.9	6.0	4.6	5.6

NOTES
^{a}In millions of 1966 colones.
^{b}Includes manufacturing and mining.
^{c}Includes electricity, gas, water, transportation, communication and storage.
^{d}Includes wholesale and retail trade, restaurants, hotels and banking.
^{e}Includes the other sectors and activities not well specified.

SOURCE
Estimates by Ministry of Labour based on Central Bank data together with refined figures from the Census and from the July 1976 Household Employment Survey.

TABLE 4.A.3 Urban and rural population distribution, labour force, employment and unemployment

	Number of persons			Relative Distribution		
	1963	*1973*	*1976*	*1963* %	*1973* %	*1976* %
Total population	1,336,000	1,879,000	2,009,000	100.0	100.0	100.0
Urban	461,000	764,000	863,000	34.5	40.6	43.0
Rural	876,000	1,116,000	1,146,000	65.5	59.4	57.0
Labour Force	395,000	588,000	658,000	100.0	100.0	100.0
Urban	146,000	255,000	301,000	37.0	43.4	45.8
Rural	249,000	333,000	357,000	63.0	56.6	54.2
Employed	368,000	545,000	617,000	100.0	100.0	100.0
Urban	134,000	239,000	281,000	36.5	43.8	45.5
Rural	234,000	306,000	336,000	63.5	56.2	54.5
Unemployed	27,500	43,300	40,900	100.0	100.0	100.0
Urban	12,000	16,500	20,400	43.6	38.2	49.8
Rural	15,500	26,700	20,500	56.4	61.8	50.2

NOTE
Details may not add to totals because of rounding.

SOURCE
Population Census, 1963 and 1973; and Household Employment Survey, July 1976.

TABLE 4.A.4   Average annual growth rates of population, labour force, employment and unemployment, 1963–76

Population, labour force and employment	1963–73 %	1973–76 %	1963–76 %
Total Population	3.5	2.3	3.2
Urban	5.2	4.2	4.9
Rural	2.5	0.9	2.1
Labour Force	4.1	3.8	4.0
Urban	5.7	5.7	5.7
Rural	2.9	2.3	2.8
Employed	4.0	4.3	4.1
Urban	5.9	5.5	5.8
Rural	2.7	3.2	2.8
Unemployed	4.7	−1.8	3.1
Urban	3.3	7.2	4.2
Rural	5.6	−8.4	2.2

SOURCE
See Table 4.A.3.

Urban poverty and economic development

TABLE 4.A.5   Age and sex composition of the labour force
(1963 and 1976)

Labour force	1963 Total	1963 Men	1963 Women	1976 Total	1976 Men	1976 Women
Labour Force	395,000	331,000	64,000	658,000	509,000	148,000
12 to 19 years	82,000	66,000	15,000	144,000	108,000	36,000
20 to 44 years	224,000	185,000	39,000	375,000	209,000	95,000
45 to 64 years	75,000	67,000	8,400	119,000	104,000	16,000
65 and over	13,000	12,000	900	18,000	16,000	1,600
Unknown	1,100	900	200	1,000	600	400
Employed	368,000	305,000	63,000	617,000	484,000	133,000
12 to 19 years	68,000	53,000	15,000	124,000	95,000	29,000
20 to 44 years	215,000	176,000	39,000	358,000	271,000	87,000
45 to 64 years	71,000	63,000	8,300	117,000	102,000	15,000
65 and over	13,000	12,000	900	17,000	16,000	1,600
Unknown	1,100	800	200	1,000	600	400
Unemployed	27,400	26,100	1,400	40,900	25,200	15,700
12 to 19 years	13,800	13,000	800	20,400	12,800	7,700
20 to 44 years	9,200	8,800	500	17,500	10,000	7,500
45 to 64 years	4,300	4,200	100	2,500	1,800	–
65 and over	–	–	–	500	500	–
Unknown	–	–	–	–	–	–

NOTE
Extensive rounding has been performed on these figures.

SOURCE
1963 Census and July 1976 Household Employment Survey.

TABLE 4.A.6 Average annual growth rates of age–sex cohorts in the labour force, 1963–76

Labour force	Total	Men	Women
Labour force	3.99	3.37	6.63
12 to 19 years	4.50	3.85	6.85
20 to 44 years	4.03	3.26	6.95
45 to 64 years	3.60	3.44	4.82
65 and over	2.49	2.31	4.70
Unknown	−0.83	−2.35	3.05
Employed	4.06	3.62	5.89
12 to 19 years	4.77	4.59	5.37
20 to 44 years	3.99	3.36	6.37
45 to 64 years	3.91	3.82	4.59
65 and over	2.26	2.05	4.70
Unknown	−0.71	−2.29	3.05
Unemployed	3.12	−0.26	20.71
12 to 19 years	3.03	−0.14	19.07
20 to 44 years	5.05	1.04	23.71
45 to 64 years	−4.28	−6.21	15.01
65 and over	43.0	43.0	–
Unknown	−3.76	−3.31	–

SOURCE
See Table 4.A.5.

TABLE 4.A.7 Employed wage earners by institutional sector and occupation—July 1976

	Total	Pro-fessionals	Tech-nicians	Admin-istrators	Clerical and sales pers.	Blue-collar workers	Service personnel	Unknown
Numbers								
Total	447,000	16,300	30,600	13,900	74,500	234,000	76,700	1,400
Central Government	48,200	7,100	15,800	1,800	9,200	6,000	8,200	200
State Enterprise	54,300	5,000	9,400	1,600	16,100	13,700	8,400	100
Private Sector	345,000	4,200	5,400	10,500	49,200	214,000	60,100	1,200
Percentages								
Total	100.0	100.0	100.0	100.0	100.0	100.0	100.0	100.0
Central Government	10.8	43.5	51.7	12.6	12.3	2.6	10.7	11.5
State Enterprise	12.1	30.6	30.7	11.8	21.6	5.9	10.9	6.5
Private Sector	77.1	25.9	17.6	75.6	66.1	91.6	78.4	81.9

NOTE
The figures in the upper half of the table have been rounded.

SOURCE
Household Employment Survey, July 1976.

TABLE 4.A.8 Employed wage earners by economic activity and occupation—July 1976

	Total	Pro-fessionals	Tech-nicians	Admini-strators and managers	Clerical and sales workers	Blue-collar workers	Service personnel	Unknown
Numbers								
Total	447,400	16,300	30,600	13,900	74,500	234,000	76,700	1,400
Agriculture	118,900	400	500	4,200	800	111,600	1,400	–
Mining & Manufacturing	73,900	1,300	800	2,000	9,800	52,400	7,200	300
Construction	32,700	300	2,800	200	1,000	27,100	1,200	100
Basic services	28,700	700	1,200	700	5,700	17,800	2,600	–
Commerce	67,700	1,400	1,700	3,500	38,600	6,100	16,100	400
Other services	122,800	11,900	23,600	3,000	18,100	18,100	47,900	200
Not well specified	2,800	200	100	200	600	1,000	200	400
Percentages								
Total	100.0	100.0	100.0	100.0	100.0	100.0	100.0	100.0
Agriculture	26.6	2.5	1.6	30.5	1.0	47.7	1.8	–
Mining & manufacturing	16.5	8.0	2.6	14.4	13.2	22.4	9.4	23.2
Construction	7.3	2.0	9.1	1.4	1.3	11.6	1.6	4.4
Basic services	6.4	4.0	3.9	5.1	7.6	7.6	3.4	2.2
Commerce	15.1	8.6	5.4	25.1	51.8	2.6	21.0	26.1
Services	27.4	73.3	77.2	21.7	24.3	7.7	62.4	15.9
Not well specified	0.6	1.5	0.2	1.9	0.8	0.4	0.3	28.2

NOTE
The figures in the upper half of the table have been rounded.

SOURCE
Household Employment Survey, July 1976.

TABLE 4.A.9 Employment by institutional sector—1950, 1973 and 1976

| | 1950 | % | 1973 | % | 1976 | % | Average annual growth rates | |
							1950-73 %	1973-76 %
Total	280,000	100.0	545,000	100.0	662,000	100.0	2.9	4.2
Private sector	263,000	93.8	458,000	84.0	514,000	83.4	2.4	3.9
Public sector[a]	17,000	6.2	87,000	16.0	102,000	16.6	7.3	5.6
Central Government	15,000	5.2	40,000	7.4	48,000	7.8	4.5	6.1
State enterprises	3,000	1.0	47,000	8.6	54,000	8.8	13.2	5.3

NOTES

The employment figures have been rounded.
[a]The public sector is composed of central government and state enterprises. Information for 1950 comes from IECES, *El Desarrollo Económico de Costa Rica, estudio No. 4, El Sector Público de la Economía Costarricense.* For 1973, CCSS, Estadísticas de Asegurados. For 1976, the July Household Employment Survey.

SOURCE
Population Census (1950 and 1973), Household Employment Survey (July 1976), and CCSS and the University of Costa Rica, as noted above.

TABLE 4.A.10 Labour force participation rates[a] by age and sex cohorts (1963 and 1976)

Ages		1963			1976	
	Total	Men	Women	Total	Men	Women
Total	29.6	49.5	9.6	32.7	50.5	14.8
12 to 19 years	35.9	58.6	13.5	34.1	50.0	17.5
20 to 44 years	58.1	97.1	20.2	61.0	94.5	29.7
45 to 64 years	54.3	95.7	12.2	51.9	88.9	13.7
65 and over	31.5	58.6	5.0	23.3	44.8	4.0
Unknown	–	–	–	75.2	77.6	71.4

NOTE
[a]Labour force as a percentage of the population belonging to that particular age–sex cohort.

SOURCE
Table 4.A.5, 1963 Census and July 1976 Household Employment Survey.

TABLE 4.A.11 Unemployment rates by age and sex cohorts (1963 and 1976)

Ages		1963			1976	
	Total %	Men %	Women %	Total %	Men %	Women %
Total	6.9	7.9	2.1	6.2	5.0	10.6
12 to 19 years	16.9	19.7	5.1	14.1	11.8	20.8
20 to 44 years	4.1	4.7	1.2	4.7	3.6	7.9
45 to 64 years	5.8	6.3	1.2	2.1	1.8	4.0
65 and over	–	–	–	3.0	3.2	–
Unknown	4.6	5.5	1.2	3.1	4.9	–

SOURCE
See Table 4.A.5.

TABLE 4.A.12   Participation rates and unemployment by region (urban and rural), 1963 and 1976

Years	Population	Labour force	Unemployed	Unemployment Rate %	Participation Rate %
1963					
Country Total	1,336,000	395,000	27,500	6.9	29.6
Rural	876,000	249,000	15,500	6.2	28.4
Urban	461,000	146,000	12,000	8.2	31.7
1973					
Country Total	1,879,000	588,000	43,300	7.4	31.3
Rural	1,116,000	333,000	26,700	8.0	29.8
Urban	764,000	255,000	16,500	6.5	33.5
1976					
Country Total	2,009,000	658,000	40,900	6.2	32.7
Rural	1,146,000	357,000	20,500	5.8	31.1
Urban	863,000	301,000	20,400	6.8	34.9

NOTE
The figures in the first three columns have been rounded.

SOURCE
See Table 4.A.3.

TABLE 4.A.13 Underemployment and its equivalent in terms of unemployment, 1967 and 1976

	Rate of equivalent unemployment		
	36-hours criterion		*47-hours criterion*
	1967 %	*1976* %	*1976* %
Total	11.4[a]	9.1[a]	6.9
Visible underemployment	4.2[a]	4.0[a]	2.8[b]
Invisible underemployment	7.2[c]	5.1[d]	4.1[e]

NOTES
[a]Persons who worked less than 36 hours per week, as a proportion of the labour force.
[b]Persons who worked less than 47 hours per week, and who wanted to work more, as a proportion of the labour force.
[c]Persons who worked 36 or more hours per week and whose income was less than ₡300 per month.
[d]Persons who worked 36 or more hours per week and who earned incomes of less then ₡600 per month, as a proportion of the labour force.
[e]Persons who worked 47 or more hours per week and who earned an income of less than ₡600 per month.

SOURCE
Household Employment Surveys, 1967 and 1976.

TABLE 4.A.14 Population, labour force and employment—July 1976

	Population	Labour force	Employed	Unemployed	Inactive population
Numbers					
Total country	2,009,000	658,000	617,000	41,000	1,352,000
Central valley	1,281,000	436,000	410,000	26,000	845,000
Metropolitan Area	549,000	196,000	184,000	12,000	353,000
Remainder of central valley	732,000	240,000	226,000	14,000	492,000
Rest of country	728,000	221,000	206,000	15,000	507,000
Percentages					
Total country	100.0	100.0	100.0	100.0	100.0
Central valley	63.8	66.3	66.5	63.5	62.5
Metropolitan Area	27.3	29.8	29.8	29.0	26.1
Remainder of central valley	36.4	36.5	36.6	34.5	36.4
Rest of country	36.2	33.7	33.5	36.4	37.5

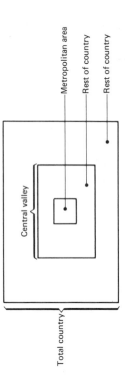

Central valley

Metropolitan area

Rest of country

Rest of country

Total country

NOTE
The figures in the upper half of the table have been rounded.

SOURCE
Household Employment Survey, July 1976.

84

TABLE 4.A.15   Participation rates[a] and unemployment rates, by location and sex—July 1976

| | Participation rate | | | Unemployment rate | | |
	Total	Men	Women	Total	Men	Women
Country Total	32.7	50.5	14.8	6.2	5.0	10.6
Central valley	34.1	–	–	6.0	–	–
Metropolitan Area	35.7	49.7	22.9	6.1	6.1	6.0
Rest of central valley	32.8	–	–	5.9	–	–
Rest of country	30.4	–	–	6.7	–	–

NOTE
[a]Uncorrected for differences in the age composition of the underlying population.

SOURCE
Household Employment Survey, July 1976.

TABLE 4.A.16   Internal migrants[a] by destination and labour force status–July 1976

| | | Labour force | | | Inactive |
Net internal migration	Popul-ation	Total	Employed	Unem-ployed	popu-lation
Metropolitan Area	512,000	196,000	184,000	12,000	316,000
Immigrants	26,000	11,000	1,000	800	15,000
% immigrants	5.1	5.8	5.8	6.6	4.7
Central valley	1,194,000	436,000	410,000	26,000	21,000
Immigrants	21,000	8,300	7,800	600	500
% immigrants	1.8	1.9	1.9	2.2	2.6
Rest of country	670,000	221,000	206,000	15,000	23,000
Immigrants	6,100	2,800	2,500	300	200
% immigrants	0.9	1.3	1.2	2.0	1.0

NOTE
The figures in the table have been rounded.
[a]Migrants are defined as those who moved during the three-year period preceding the survey date.

SOURCE
Household Employment Survey, July 1976.

Urban poverty and economic development

ΤABLE 4.A.17   Average monthly salary (in Costa Rican colones) by region–
July 1976

Region	Total	Urban	Rural	Urban/ rural ratio
Country Total	1090	1377	800	1.72
Metropolitan Area	1464	1497	1306	1.15
Central valley	1156	1406	799	1.76
Remainder of country	928	1234	802	1.54

SOURCE
Ministry of Labor and Social Security and Ministry of Economy, Industry and
Commerce; Household Employment Survey, July 1976.

TABLE 4.A.18   Sectoral contribution to labour absorption in the country as
a whole, 1973 and 1976

Sector	Employment			Relative composition		
	1973	1976	1973-76 increase	1973 %	1976 %	1973-76 increase %
Total country	542,000	617,000	74,000	100.0	100.0	100.0
Agriculture	207,000	215,000	7,400	38.2	34.8	9.9
Industry and manufacturing	70,000	90,000	20,500	12.9	14.6	27.5
Construction	37,000	40,000	2,800	6.9	6.5	3.8
Basic services[a]	30,000	34,000	4,600	5.5	5.6	6.1
Commerce[b]	79,000	100,000	21,100	14.7	16.3	28.3
Personal services[c]	117,000	133,000	16,100	21.6	21.6	21.6
Others[d]	1,200	3,200	2,100	0.2	0.5	2.8

NOTES
The figures in the first three columns of the table have been rounded.
[a]Includes electricity, gas, water, transportation, storage and communication.
[b]Includes wholesale and retail trade, hotels, restaurants and banking.
[c]Includes social, community and personal services.
[d]Includes activities not well specified and unknown.

SOURCE
Household Employment Survey, July 1976.

TABLE 4.A.19 Sectoral contribution to labour absorption in the Metropolitan Area of San José

Sector	Level of employment					
	Numbers			Percentages		
	1973	1976	1973-76 increase	1973	1976	1973-76 increase
Total Metropolitan Area	161,000	184,000	24,000	100.0	100.0	100.0
Industry and manufacturing	35,000	43,000	7,600	21.9	23.2	32.2
Construction	13,000	14,000	1,000	8.2	7.6	4.3
Basic services[a]	11,000	10,000	200	6.6	5.7	1.0
Commerce[b]	40,000	51,000	10,400	25.2	27.6	43.9
Personal services[c]	56,000	60,000	4,300	34.6	32.5	18.0
Others[d]	5,600	6,200	600	3.5	3.4	2.6

NOTE
The numbers in the first three columns of the table have been rounded.
[a]Includes electricity, gas, water, transportation, storage and communication.
[b]Includes wholesale and retail trade, hotels, restaurants and banking.
[c]Includes social, community and personal services.
[d]Includes activities not well specified and unknown.

SOURCE
Household Employment Survey, July 1976.

88   *Urban poverty and economic development*

TABLE 4.A.20   Equivalent unemployment rates by under-employment
types–July 1976

Type of underemployment	Whole country %	San José Metropolitan Area %	Other urban %	Rural %
Visible				
(i) Relative to employed population	3.0	1.5	2.4	3.4
(ii) Relative to labour force	2.8	1.4	2.2	3.3
Invisible				
Relative to labour force	4.1	3.6	3.6	4.4
Total unemployment equivalent (relative to labour force)	6.9	5.0	5.8	7.7
Open unemployment rate	6.2	6.1	6.8	5.8
Total unemployment rate (open plus equivalent from under-employment)	13.1	11.1	12.6	13.5

SOURCE
Household Employment Survey, July 1976.

APPENDIX II   DATA SOURCES FROM THE *TUGURIO* SURVEY

One data source used in this study deserves a brief description. The sample survey of *tugurio* households and adults was a one-time effort by the Oficina de Información's Public Opinion Unit. Coordinating a multiagency set of interests in information about these neighbourhoods, the Office sampled 575 families, containing 2970 persons in the San José *tugurios*. A separate survey, conducted at the same time, used a more detailed questionnaire with randomly chosen adults from the same districts, and achieved usable interview data for 517.

The sample was randomly drawn in neighbourhoods previously identified by the National Housing Agency (INVU) as deteriorated. In addition to evidence of physical conditions of housing and existence or lack of urban infrastructural services, the Agency relied on 1973 census tract data that dealt with income, unemployment, educational attainment, and home ownership. A point system was assigned to these indicators. One hundred and eight zones were labelled 'deteriorated', using this point system, and forty-one fell into the areas of greatest deterioration. The sampling was done from these forty-one zones.

The survey was undertaken in the field during the months of May and June 1977. The census of 1973 had been carried out in May. A comparable employment survey of households was done in July 1976. Fortunately, these periods of the year were sufficiently comparable to avoid problems of seasonal variation.

Of the two surveys, the household survey was oriented most strongly towards housing, family size, and family composition. The adult survey, by contrast, tried to focus on behaviour, experience, aspirations, attitudes, and preferences of the respondents.

The sample survey of the *tugurios* was stratified according to three types of *tugurios*: concentrated, dispersed, and 'unstable pockets'. The latter was in turn subdivided into two types, according to whether the pockets were located on state-owned or privately owned land. Numbers of interviews in these four strata were approximately proportional to the estimated population in each. Detailed descriptions of the 'collective personalities' of each of these types appear in Chapter 7, Social and Historical Approaches to Poverty Assessment.

A more detailed description of the sample and survey methods and the problems encountered is contained in a mimeographed publication of the Oficina de Información, 'Informe preliminar de la encuesta en zonas marginales de Area Metropolitana de San José – 1977 – Aspectos metodológicos'. The publication is marked 'Distribución Restringida; Primer borrador – Agosto 1977'.

5 Poverty assessment: six approaches

Poverty is not homogeneous, unidimensional, or monolithic. Its perceived nature varies among countries and cultures, according to levels of 'subsistence' and consumption, influenced by methods of measurement, and guided by basic assumptions about human nature, social justice, and the possibility of basic change. Poverty is perceived through the screen of a variety of competing theoretical models and the imperfections of empirical data. Campaigns against poverty provide insight into society's notions of its causes and into the intensity of our desire to maintain or alleviate it.

Clearly, no single definition or characterisation of such a complex phenomenon will satisfy every purpose. Instead, we want to draw on a menu of definitions, applicable to different strategies, opportunities, and justifications for intervention.

This chapter surveys briefly a range of approaches to thinking about and measuring poverty. Concepts of poverty should be as rich and variegated as the cultural, economic, and political realities that cause it, constrain its solutions, and influence the design of effective interventions.

For the most part, the different approaches to understanding poverty outlined below are complementary concepts rather than competitive ones. We start with conventional concepts and work toward less familiar characterisations, involving more elaborate theories, assumptions, and analyses. As might be anticipated, each approach has relative advantages and drawbacks, and each brings along with it a typical constituency of users and advocates.

The first set of definitions focus on poverty lines. In order of their presentation, they are:

1. Per capita income
2. Market basket estimates of poverty lines
3. Income distribution measures

In general, these are relatively easy to conceive and measure, but they tend to represent symptoms and outcomes, rather than refer to conditions of poverty, its causes, and policies that might fight it.

A second set of characterisations refer to poverty conditions and processes. They include:

4. Social indicators
5. Access to social and economic capital
6. Poverty in historical perspective

Each demands more of analysis than do the first three, and not surprisingly, each yields greater potential guidance for policy.

1 AVERAGE PER CAPITA INCOME

The arithmetic quotient of gross national product or national income, divided by the number of a country's inhabitants, is the most widely quoted measure of a country's average wealth or poverty. It is well accepted, easily measured, and readily understood.

Its drawbacks are also well known by now. It is conspicuously silent about the distribution of income, so that countries where the majority are very poor may nevertheless have a relatively high average income per capita. The arithmetic mean of an income distribution can be skewed upwards by the presence of even a few very high income recipients.

Less crucial are problems associated with international comparisons, sensitive as they are to the proper choice of exchange rates. Beyond this, a given level of money income per capita may spell poverty in one set of circumstances and comfort in another, depending on cultural expectations, the degree of urbanisation, the extent of self-reliance, role of unmeasured income items, and the basic accuracy of the national income aggregates themselves.

2 MARKET BASKET ESTIMATES OF POVERTY LINES

International comparisons of poverty are furthered by the designation of a standard market basket of goods and services, thought to represent minimum consumption standards, and the pricing of the total contents of the basket. Actual local costs of food, clothing, housing and other basic necessities lie at the base of this method. The measurement focuses directly on the specific material needs of poor people, which requires a set of explicit value judgements. It provides reasonably reliable estimates of the income required to purchase minimum market baskets of these goods. The standards may fluctuate by family size and by urban and rural residence. The US Department of Labor's Bureau of Labor Statistics is only one of a number of national statistical agencies that has found such calculations useful.

The market basket estimates discussed here and in the following chapter are narrower than the International Labour Office's basic needs approach. In addition to the material goods purchased out of family incomes, basic needs include as well minimum standards of public services together with the desire that the 'needs' be socially and politically determined, rather than handed down by an authority or a group of experts.[1]

The market basket method is not without its disadvantages. Very briefly, they include:

(a) the variation in individual and family behaviour in spending a minimum income in an optimal way. Poor people with the statistical minimum income may consume a basket of goods considered suboptimal by poverty analysts in government agencies. They may value special recreational interests, or unusual medical expenditures, or minor pleasures such as cigarettes, more highly than they care for nutritious low-cost food. In short, the measurement rejects any notion of consumer sovereignty.

(b) the changing definition of the contents of the minimum basket. Bicycles and transistor radios might be luxuries at an early point in the development of a particular village, but key elements in a later economic development strategy.

(c) the costs of specifying and pricing the basket's components. Dietary requirements, local buying habits, and current prices are required.

3 INCOME DISTRIBUTION MEASURES

Measurement of income distribution looks at poverty as a relative concept, focusing on persons who fall into the lower deciles, say, of the income receivers, without specifying their income either in money or in terms of its power to purchase minimum market baskets. The notion of relative deprivation suggests that persons at the base of the income distributional pyramid are disadvantaged no matter what their absolute income might be. According to this school, their sense of well being is determined largely by the gaps perceived between their own status and others with whom they compare themselves. In this spirit, some surveys suggest that people accept income differentials as 'just', provided that the worst off do not fall more than halfway below the average income for the population as a whole.[2] An implicit theory of social justice is at work here. Either an acculturated or a logically argued sense of 'fair' differences among people is implicitly compared with the greater, 'unfair' differences that ought to be corrected.

Some see the presence of an implicit theory of social justice as a disadvantage, weakening the usefulness of income distributional measures. They would prefer to deal with poverty as an objective problem without having to tangle with the problems of social philosophy. Others argue that the use of income distributional measures eventually forces policy makers to be explicit about ideological assumptions that inevitably enter into any consideration of poverty problems.

Relative income shares have been measured in a wide variety of rich and poor countries.[3] The necessary data are routinely generated in population censuses. The semi-median income level mentioned earlier is not widely used as an upper bound to poverty-level incomes, although it corresponds closely to other measures of poverty and may be easier to compute, say, than Gini coefficients or Kuznets indices. More common are references to relative income shares in the context of defining specific target groups for poverty policy. For example, a housing programme might be designed to reach the third or fourth (but not the first and second) income deciles from the bottom. Such a strategy would avoid people with the lowest incomes, deemed unable to make even minimal mortgage payments, as well as those in the middle income brackets, adequately served by conventional housing lenders.

4 SOCIAL INDICATORS

The use of social indicators shifts attention away from income to conditions of poverty present in the social environment. Data refer to housing, community facilities, health and educational services, mortality and morbidity rates, transportation needs, communications media, and other public goods that bear on the collective needs of the poor.

Such measures sometimes require ad hoc surveys of conditions, community by community. Standards of 'minimum' public services are not yet a matter of consensus, although some have been suggested by United Nations studies, work by the ILO on basic needs, and other literature on community development. One school of thought holds that priority needs and development strategies cannot be formulated beforehand, or in the abstract, but only in response to particular local conditions, and convincing expressions of community commitment towards specific objectives.[4] Other groups have taken a less extreme position in trying to design contingency strategies adapted to local circumstances. For example, housing policies may distinguish between groups best served by the provision of minimal sites and services, and those better organised groups able to undertake mutual aid programmes, or individuals already tied into main-stream economic activity who can meet monthly payments on government-built houses.[5]

5 ACCESS TO ECONOMIC AND SOCIAL CAPITAL

The poverty problem can be addressed in terms of access to capital, as the chief point of leverage for poor people to generate economic progress for themselves. Emphasis shifts from income flows to capital stocks, from 'market basket' categories of subsistence and consumption to social leverage for change.

The nature of capital assets is not always clearly agreed upon, however. Some treatments of poverty are focused on *economic* capital, including credit, land, and human capital, or education. Other analyses give more attention to *social institutions* that help to mobilise the untapped resources of initiative, underemployed labour, and collective efforts that exist even in the most downtrodden communities. Here one can cite the role of cooperatives, community development corporations, technical assistance networks, grass roots political movements, and government-sponsored campaigns. Even specialised organisations such as volunteer fire companies or soccer teams have been known to take on broader functions under special circumstances such as earthquake relief, or fund-raising for development projects. Also included may be the basic apparatus of democratic decision-making, including popular participation in mutual-aid projects. Measures of capital stocks as indicators of potential to break out of poverty have the advantage of providing a clearer picture of the context which mediates the effectiveness of other policies designed as poverty-intervention programmes.

There are also disadvantages of this approach. Policies to create social and economic capital for change are generally more difficult to implement than delivery of more specific goods and services. Designing the appropriate forms of capital and social institutions is likely to raise political questions that go beyond the scope of conventional technical assistance. Needs will vary from one community to another, and different communities are likely to have their own different priorities and views of what is possible. Basic ingredients necessary for success, such as entrepreneurship, territorial identity, or managerial skills may be missing, and difficult to inject through public programmes alone. Despite these problems, a considerable body of development literature concludes these social-psychological and political-institutional dimensions of poverty must be faced and dealt with explicitly if poverty interventions are to have any appreciable chance of success.[6]

6 POVERTY IN HISTORICAL PERSPECTIVE

Poverty can be viewed in broad, long-term historical perspective. In this view, heavier reliance is placed on interpretive theory rather than on narrow empirical measurement of functional relationships in specific communities. Attention rests on major contextual events and forces affecting the status of broad social classes. Among these are wars, political revolutions, technological breakthroughs, ideological sensitisation and subsequent mobilisation of efforts on a sustained basis; major moves to exploit previously untapped natural resources, shifts in world markets and in international investment propensities, and confluences of long-term trends that bring (or could bring) poor people into the mainstream of development.

One can point to a number of examples. World War II affected technological development, brought the West out of the Great Depression, and ended the era of direct colonial ties. More recently, awareness of global limits to growth has increased, based on projected exhaustion of physical resources. Ecological catastrophe is quietly spreading, especially in large areas of Africa and South America. Striking changes in agriculture, transportation, communications, marketing, and other technologies are creating major shifts in control over productive processes, and in the incidence of benefits from economic development. New ideological movements are emerging in the field of technical assistance, calling for greater self-reliance, more appropriate technology, efforts oriented towards basic needs, and policies of solidarity among Third World countries to cartelise their mineral resources.

The historical approach to analysis of poverty's causes and cures is acknowledged to contain more problems than the five perspectives cited earlier. Nevertheless, we feel that it deserves attention here. Neglect of poverty's historical perspective will lead to policy failure, both in developing countries and in stagnant regions of more advanced nations.

Despite the pitfalls of historical analysis, we believe it is both a useful and feasible ingredient of policy formulation in technical assistance. An obvious and relatively unexplored place to start lies in the comparative analysis of case studies of successful anti-poverty strategies in the past. Evaluation of past success and failure broadens attention from narrow reductionist models of development to a fuller account of the long-term processes of social transformation that must accompany effective poverty interventions.

The next two chapters will address the six major approaches to poverty assessment in turn, beginning with the relatively straightforward consideration of per capita income levels, and ending with the more problematic application of historical models. In each case, reference will be made to Costa Rican data as an illustrative context.

Throughout this comparative review, we will continue to give special attention to the characteristics of poverty that are seen to be confined within particular spatial entities, or alternatively, are thought to flow across spatial boundaries, thus calling for tools of analysis both broader in geographic scope and richer in theoretical content.

The next chapter, Chapter 6, deals with the first three approaches to poverty assessment, namely, (1) average income per capita, (2) the income equivalent of minimum consumption standards, and (3) income distribution. All are essentially concerned with measurements of money income or income equivalents. The subsequent chapter, Chapter 7, takes up the remaining three approaches. These relate more broadly to social institutions and processes, namely, (4) social indicators, (5) access to capital, and (6) poverty in its historical perspective. The first of the two chapters will be relatively brief because it treats fairly well-defined and broadly accepted categories of economic measurement. The second is more extensive, treating the less conventional social and historical approaches.

6 Poverty assessment through income measures

This chapter discusses three approaches to conceptualisation and measurement of poverty, all revolving around the measurement of monetary incomes. In the previous chapter, we made brief comparisons among these approaches, as well as comparison between these income measures of poverty and the broader, less conventional social and historical approaches to poverty assessment. We now turn to a more detailed review of each of the income approaches, saving the social and historical analysis for the next chapter. In order to make the analysis concrete, empirical observations from Costa Rica, centring in metropolitan San José, are used illustratively throughout.

1 PER CAPITA INCOME LEVELS AND THE SPATIAL DISTRIBUTION OF POVERTY

Is poverty in recognised slum areas, *tugurios*, markedly different, in terms of per capita income, from poverty in other urban areas? The answer affects the design of poverty intervention strategies. If slums are spatial concentrations of poverty, then appropriate policies would naturally focus on them as self-contained problems. Seen this way, the issue of poverty is visible, associated with clearly defined locations of physical deterioration. Depiction of the poor as predominately slum dwellers also makes poverty more tractable. As exceptions to the general picture of urban progress, slums can be treated separately from the larger urban, national, or global environment that may have caused slum conditions. This view assumes that poverty has neither significant roots nor serious manifestations beyond the slums themselves.

Tugurios have been defined and identified in San José in

accordance with a systematic reconnaissance carried out by the National Housing Institute (INVU) using a variety of devices including census data, special surveys, aerial photography and field observations. The definitions of a *tugurio* was based on a weighted formula of social, economic and physical characteristics, with most weight given to physical characteristics and least weight to social factors. Using these criteria, in 1976 INVU identified 118 *tugurios* in the San José Metropolitan Area. It should be noted that if stronger weight were given to social and economic factors, it is possible that other *tugurio* areas might be identified, especially since socio-economic deprivation can easily exist hidden behind the facade of decent physical exteriors.

Using the INVU studies, analysts of the Costa Rican Office of Planning and Economic Policy (OFIPLAN) made a broad distinction among three types of *tugurios*:

I *Concentrated* slums, generally originating in the post-war period of the late 1940s.
II *Dispersed* areas of shacks and shantytowns, formed more recently during the 1960s.
III *Unstable pockets* of isolated poverty, with diverse ages and origins.

Figure 6.1 gives a general idea of the location and extent of *tugurio* poverty in the Metropolitan Area in 1973: an estimated 73,000 (15 per cent) lived in *tugurios*. Not all residents were poor, however, and not all the poor were in the *tugurios*. Many could be found elsewhere in the city. How many poor are counted in each place depends on where one draws the poverty line in terms of minimum income levels.

Table 6.1 summarises the distribution and intensity of poverty in metropolitan San José, based on two alternative estimates of 'minimum' per capita annual income at ₡2,000 and ₡1,300 respectively. These figures designate a 'minimum' income based on market basket calculations explained later in the chapter.

The table underscores a significant finding: *income profiles did not differ greatly between tugurio and non-tugurio areas of San José.* Using the ₡2,000 poverty line definition, about half (55 per cent) of the people in *tugurios* were 'poor', but roughly a third (33 per cent) of the people living in the rest of the Metropolitan Area were also poor. The same picture emerged using the more stringent ₡1,300 poverty line: by this definition, 32 per cent of

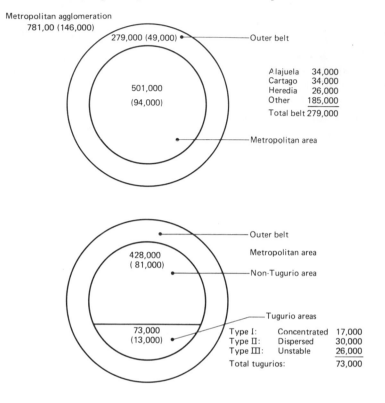

FIG   6.1.   Population   data   (1973)   for   San   José   –   Urban
Agglomeration. Metropolitan Area, and *tugurio* areas
[Number of families shown in brackets]

tugurio residents had incomes lower than theoretical subsistence requirements, and 18 per cent of other people in other areas of San José fell into the same category. The relative concentration of poverty inside and outside *tugurios* was about the same regardless of which poverty line was used. That is, the ratio of non-*tugurio*/*tugurio* poverty concentrations was about the same using the ₡2,000 benchmark ($\frac{33}{55} = 0.60$) or the ₡1,300 benchmark ($\frac{18}{32} = 0.56$).

All these statistics indicate that, contrary to the usual views of poverty as mainly focused in slums, poverty in San José was highly dispersed throughout the Metropolitan Area. Referring to columns

TABLE 6.1 Distribution and intensity of poverty in San José

1973 Census data	Population (1)	Population as percentage of total (2)	The poor: annual per capita income				The poor as percentage of all inhabitants of the area, poverty defined at	
			Below ₡2000 No. (3)	% (4)	Below ₡1300 No. (5)	% (6)	₡2000 (7)=(3÷1)	₡1300 (8)=(5÷1)
Column:								
Total population of San José Metropolitan Area	501,000	100	181,000	100	99,000	100	36	20
Tugurio areas	73,000	15	40,000	22	23,000	23	55	32
Non-tugurio areas	428,000	85	141,000	78	76,000	77	33	18

NOTE

Income figures shown here for San José residents may be underestimated in one respect that deserves note. Census takers estimated annual incomes on the basis of information solicited concerning income in the month preceding the census survey (for 1973, this was the month of May). Many San José residents, however, received supplementary income during the coffee harvest months (October–January), given the close proximity of coffee farms to the city. Most of these earnings were probably not reflected in the census-reported earnings. Unfortunately, the magnitude of earnings for the particular groups addressed in this study are not known. This distortion in the data would mean that the *absolute* number of people shown living below poverty lines in table 6.1 are likely to be exaggerated, perhaps by as much as a few percentage points. Nevertheless, this would apply to San José as a whole, and would not necessarily affect the estimated *spatial distribution* of poor people as between *tugurios* and non-*tugurio* parts of the Metropolitan Area. We have no evidence that coffee harvesters came predominantly from the *tugurios*, but if this were the case, it would contribute disproportionate additional incomes to *tugurio* residents not recorded in the May census. This would strengthen the tentative conclusions we draw from the data (discussed further below), namely that slums are not very distinctive from other parts of the Metropolitan Area in terms of income profiles or concentrations of poverty.

SOURCE
1973 census of population.

3 to 6 of the table, it appears that the great majority of poor people (defined by whatever choice of poverty line) were located outside areas identified as *tugurios*. More specifically, Table 6.1 shows that *tugurios* contained 23 per cent of people living below the ₡1,300 level and 22 per cent of those living below the ₡2,000 level. By either definition of poverty, therefore, more than three-quarters of the poor were scattered elsewhere in the Metropolitan Area.

Reference to Table 6.2 provides another insight into the tenuous overlap between poverty boundaries and slum boundaries. Fully 46 per cent of those living in *tugurios* were not poor by the ₡2,000-level definition, while 68 per cent were above the ₡1,300 subsistence level. Elsewhere in the city, 33 per cent were below the ₡2,000 poverty level and 18 per cent below ₡1,300.

TABLE 6.2   Poverty boundaries and slum boundaries

| Area | Proportion of population receiving annually | | | |
	Below ₡1300 %	Below ₡2000 %	Above ₡2000 %	Total %
Entire Metropolitan Area	20	36	64	100
Tugurio	32	54	46	100
Non-*tugurio*	18	33	67	100

Policy implications

While it is true that some poverty can be dealt with by focusing on slums as entire units – through housing projects, slum eradication, community development programmes, and other area-specific measures – nevertheless, three-quarters of the poor will have to be reached through projects that seek out and serve the poor through comprehensive, sensitively-tuned programmes operating on a far wider spatial horizon than slums.

In Costa Rica, two steps towards this end deserve consideration. The applicability of these suggestions to other low-income countries should be clear, allowing for differences in organisation details. The first suggests a collaborative effort to be undertaken by several Costa Rican agencies in the Metropolitan Area beyond the 118 *tugurios* already identified by the National Housing

Institute (INVU). The other logically complementary approach would be to secure the cooperation of Costa Rican institutions which already deal with poverty problems, not on the basis of whole communities, but at the level of families and individuals. Costa Rica presents good opportunities for this, due to the well advanced state of social services in nutrition, social security, education and other outreach efforts focusing on the individual. An important element of this strategy would be to identify different packages of assistance which best serve the different categories of poverty being addressed by each 'poverty locating' agency. For example, nutrition programmes probably reach out to individuals at the lower end of the poverty spectrum. Such individuals are often not in a position to make good use of regular training programmes, or to qualify for small loans, or support payments on a house, or hold down a steady job. But a different package of services might serve them well: basic literacy and numeracy training provision of basic sites and services in lieu of finished houses, employment in public works rather than on an assembly line, child care services, counselling and referral services that may be needed to deal with special problems such as alcoholism and mental deficiency.

Along these lines, a Washington, D.C. consulting firm, Planning and Development Collaborative International (PADCO), has suggested that broad categories of poverty syndromes imply differentiated packages of integrated services.[1] These could be targeted through appropriate agencies, whose usual (but more specialised) outreach functions would serve as 'poverty locators' on the fine-grain scale necessary both within and outside *tugurios*. For example, education agencies may be able to help identify appropriate locations for employment generation projects and/or given references on individuals whose reliability and earning potential makes them favourable recipients of down-payment housing. Agencies dealing with environmental health problems might similarly help pinpoint efficient location of medical services to serve the non-*tugurio* poor. More work is necessary, however, to design appropriate packages of services (for example, through factor analysis) which might be appropriate to identify syndromes of needs and absorptive capacity for a diversity of services. Additional study is also needed to pick the appropriate 'locator' agencies for each package.

Even within the *tugurios*, there would be problems in effectively reaching the target group: first, nearly half of *tugurio* residents were above the upper poverty line·of ₡2,000 (compared with the rest of the city, where two-thirds were above this line). Second, 59 per cent of *tugurio* residents who fell below the ₡2,000 line also fell below the 'subsistence' line of ₡1,300, and these may have been in such desperate straits that they lacked the absorptive capacity for *conventional* poverty programmes like housing, manufacturing employment opportunities, training programmes, and other projects which demand well fed, motivated, disciplined, socially adaptable, and consistently productive individuals. It is not to imply that poverty programmes should be focused on other groups. Rather, very imaginative, well coordinated, and sensitively adapted programmes will be called for – whether in *tugurios* or in other urban areas.

2 POVERTY LINES: MARKET BASKET ESTIMATES

As part of this study, two poverty benchmarks were calculated for each of three geographic areas. They were intended to distinguish two levels of deprivation ('poverty' and 'subsistence') in the San José Metropolitan Area, in other urban areas, and in rural areas in Costa Rica.

The urban *poverty line* was based on a basket of goods and services that permitted a nuclear family of 5.3 persons to satisfy its basic needs, taking into account the level of development of the country and the consumption habits of its population. The basket included a nutritionally adequate diet, minimal clothing, modest housing, transport, and some entertainment. It did not include money to improve the educational level of family members through high school or university.

The urban *subsistence level* is roughly one-third lower than the poverty line. The basket of goods comprising this line provided family members only minimal food, housing, and clothing requirements, with almost nothing for transport or recreation.

Poverty and subsistence lines reflecting differing consumption patterns and prices were also calculated for rural and urban populations outside of the San José Metropolitan Area. The values of all poverty lines in 1973 and 1977 prices (in per capita terms) are given below:

	1973		1977	
	Poverty ₡	Subsistence ₡	Poverty ₡	Subsistence ₡
Metropolitan Area	2000	1300	3500	2300
Other urban areas	1800	1200	3200	2100
Rural areas	1200	800	2100	1400

Focusing now on the figures for the Metropolitan Area, these are translated into US dollar equivalents in Table 6.3. Note that owing both to inflation and to changes in the exchange rate, the level of money income (denominated in dollars) sufficient to purchase the poverty-line market basket in 1973 would be capable only of buying the lower, subsistence basket in 1977.

TABLE 6.3   Poverty line estimates for the San José Metropolitan Area

	1973 (₡7.6 = US$ 1)		1977 (₡8.54 = US$ 1)	
	Poverty	Subsistence	Poverty	Subsistence
Annual income	$263	$170	$410	$269
Monthly income	$22	$14	$34	$22
Daily income	$0.73	$0.47	$1.13	$0.75

Composition of market baskets

For the San José Metropolitan Area, these poverty and subsistence lines were composed of the following categories of expenditures:

	1973		1977	
	Poverty ₡	Subsistence ₡	Poverty ₡	Subsistence ₡
Food	949	720	1609	1238
Clothing	112	83	189	140
Housing	677	440	1300	847
Personal hygiene	67	27	92	34
Recreation and transport	192	32	329	60
	1997	1302	3519	2319

The food requirements in the poverty line calculations were based on a study of minimum calorie and protein needs in Costa Rica carried out by the Nutrition Institute for Central American and Panama (INCAP). This study specified an expenditure figure about 30 per cent lower than another study done by the University of Costa Rica – thereby implying that the calculation of food requirements were indeed minimal.

The San José subsistence income of US 47 cents per day had to take care of everything – food, clothing, shelter, and other basic necessities. Some items provided by the state were not included. Education is an obvious example, but in Costa Rica, medical care also fell into this category, since in principle medical services are free and universally provided.

Family income poverty lines, 1977 prices

As noted earlier, data for this study refer mainly to 1973, a census year that preceded the economic distortions of 1974–6 when the oil crisis, transitory inflation, and economic repercussions were present. Nevertheless, it is useful to note that the poverty levels defined above represent, in terms of family income rather than per capita income, and in terms of 1977 prices rather than 1973 prices, annual incomes of ₡12,190 ($1,400) and ₡18,550 ($2,200) respectively. This assumes an average family of 5.3 members and takes account of the observed price changes between 1973 and 1977 on individual items in the market basket. In general, the subsistence level income in 1977 allowed a family in a month to pay ₡263 ($31) for rent; consume less than 19 pounds of meat and fish and 20 pounds of rice; buy ₡62 ($7) of clothing; but not go to movies or other (purchased) recreation.

Common problems in defining poverty lines

While not every problem associated with this concept should be the object of worry, some do merit our specific concern:

(a) Problems of interpretation are posed when a substantial number of people live at incomes below those specified as 'minimum'. For any non-negligible proportion of the population to earn incomes lower than a subsistence amount is almost a contradiction in terms. It may mean that information on incomes is simply incomplete, with underdeclaration the rule. People may be receiving unrecorded transfers from government agencies, loans from friends and relatives, or the proceeds of illicit or illegal activities. It may mean as well that the analyst's preconceptions about minimum needs are wrong. It could also indicate that the group of people in truly desperate straits is so large that conventional poverty programmes providing education, housing, employment and health may be unable to help even if the poor could be reached. Alcoholism, mental deficiency, criminal pathology, transitory personal crises, victimisation by unpredictable events such as natural disasters or eradication programmes, untreatable illness or debilitation, death of spouse in a large family – all these problems arise in most societies and they cannot be readily treated simply by lifting people from just below to just above the poverty line.

(b) For at least some policy purposes, it is not necessary to know the money incomes of the target group. What matters is whether people are deficient in particular ways upon which agencies are prepared to act (health, housing, nutrition, jobs).

(c) Census tabulations of incomes typically underestimate income in kind, including free government services such as child nutritional programmes, subsidised housing credits, and health benefits.

(d) Different choices of poverty lines naturally affect how many people are called 'poor', but the identification of geographic concentrations of poor people will not usually be affected greatly by the choice. For example, within San José, the distribution of 'poor' people as between *tugurios* and non-*tugurio* areas is virtually the same, whether one uses the ₡1,300 ('subsistence') figure or the ₡2,000 ('poverty') figure. The same is true for size of family and education levels. Certain other variables, such as unemployment rates, dependency ratios, and housing conditions, are more sensitive to choice of poverty line.

(e) Finally, in any given year, business cycles or abnormal economic events can shift many people above or below the poverty level. People living at the margin of poverty are likely to be precariously or sporadically employed on a 'last hired, first fired' basis. Costa Rica enjoyed fairly steady growth in the period 1963–8 (marked by a 7.2 per cent average annual increase in domestic product), carrying over to a similar rise in the next five-year period (7.1 per cent from 1968 to 1973). Immediately after the 1973 census, however, there was a sharp economic downturn (growth during 1973–6 averaged only 4.0 per cent), accompanied by inflation and rising minimum wages. In that recession many people were undoubtedly dismissed from marginal jobs and slipped below the poverty line.

3 RELATIVE INCOME SHARES: INTERNATIONAL COMPARISONS

One way to describe poverty follows observation of relative income shares among population deciles. These data are readily available for most countries, either from census sources or special studies. Although income data are notoriously unreliable, some distortions cancel out in the course of making international comparisons or looking at changes over time. While it is also true that income is only a crude measure of welfare, a lack of income among the poorest groups is a sign of other basic deficiencies. This is true especially for the urban poor, who live in a specialised monetised economy, and therefore have less recourse to living off the land.

Interpretation of relative income shares usually involves international comparisons. In the case of Costa Rica, we can compare the income share of the poor – say, the lowest four income deciles – with the relative share received by the same group in other lesser developed countries (LDCs). In making this comparison, Table 6.4 shows data from the 1960s compiled by Adelman and Morris (1973) covering Costa Rica and forty-two other LDCs.[2]

The figures show that Costa Rica's poorest 40 per cent have not, in fact, done exceptionally well, when measured against the performance of other low-income countries. This is somewhat surprising, given the noteworthy efforts of the Costa Rican government to serve the disadvantaged.

Owing to the many statistical, conceptual, political, and ethical problems in making such comparisons, the specific figures themselves should not be considered exact. Table 6.5 illustrates Costa Rican deviations from the 'median experience' of the other forty-two LDCs based mainly on the data from the 1960s. This

TABLE 6.4 Relative income shares: Costa Rica and 42 other LDCs–
(Estimated percentage shares of income received by population percentiles)

Population percentiles	0-40	40-60	60-80	80-100
Costa Rica (percentage share) 1961	13.30	12.10	14.60	60.00
Median for 42 other LDCs	14.00	11.25	16.70	57.10
Range for ⎰Lowest Countries	0.50	1.28	8.72	42.00
other 42 LDCs ⎱Highest Countries	23.00	17.00	26.37	89.50
Rank of Costa Rica among other 42	24th	16th	36th	16th
Other countries of interest for				
comparison with Costa Rica:				
Bolivia (1968)	12.90	13.70	14.30	59.10
Chile (1968)	15.00	12.00	20.70	52.30
Libya (1962)	0.50	1.28	8.72	89.50
South Africa (1965)	6.11	10.16	26.37	57.36
Israel (1957)	16.00	17.00	23.90	43.10
Japan (1962)	15.30	15.80	22.90	46.00
Chad (1958)	23.00	12.00	22.00	43.00
Tanzania (1964)	19.50	9.75	9.75	61.00
Mexico (1963)	10.50	11.25	20.21	58.04
Venezuela (1962)	13.40	16.60	22.90	47.10
India (1957)	20.00	16.00	22.00	42.00

SOURCE
Adapted from Adelman and Morris (1973) p. 152. The source of Costa Rican data cited by Adelman and Morris is CEPAL, 1969, but the original source of these data appears to be a 1961 study of households limited to the San José region.

TABLE 6.5 Relative income shares

Group: Percentiles	Lowest 0-40	Middle 40-60	Upper Middle 60-80	Rich 80-100	Total
Costa Rica	13.30	12.10	14.60	60.00	100.0
'Median LDC experience'	14.00	11.25	16.70	57.10	100.0
Costa Rica as percentage of median	95	108	87	105	–

SOURCE
Adapted from Adelman and Morris (1973) p. 152

information can lead to working hypotheses on major social forces at work in Costa Rica, that poverty intervention strategies need to take into account.

The meaning of the size distribution of income can be clarified by looking at the pattern in other selected countries (see Table 6.4). We note that Costa Rica's income distribution was closely similar to Bolivia's, although Costa Rica was more like Chile in terms of other development indicators. The poor were relatively worse off in countries whose wealth derives from extractive resources – Libya, South Africa.

The poorest 20 per cent in Costa Rica can be compared with more advanced countries on the basis of other data.[3] The poorest 20 per cent of Costa Rica's population (by household) have 5.4 per cent of the income. The poorest 20 per cent in East Germany have 10.4 per cent; in Japan 8.8 per cent; Canada 6.7; Israel 5.8; Sweden 5.2; USA 3.9; France 2.3. Among Latin American countries, Guatemala's poorest 20 per cent have 8.9 of the income reported; Argentina 6.9; Chile 4.8; Mexico 4.2; Colombia 3.5; Venezuela 2.7; Ecuador and Peru both 1.8. These data confirm the pattern stated earlier: Costa Rica's poor receive income shares comparable to Latin American standards or even US standards; but they do not justify complacency, given the performance of other countries, and the degree to which the government of Costa Rica has committed itself to serving the poor.

Countries with income distribution most favourable to the poorest 40 per cent are found both in preindustrial societies (Chad, Tanzania) and in advanced industrial countries (Israel, Japan).[4] During the intervening transition, the lowest decile suffer, not only in relative terms, but often in terms of absolute loss in income, typically for one or two generations. At the dates covered by our data, Costa Rica seemed to be in this 'trough' stage of bad times for the poor. One might well ask: is the bottom of the trough still ahead? Or are the poor beginning to climb out of it? The facts from Adelman's study only represent a static snapshot taken in 1961. Available data for the years 1961 and 1971 help shed light on changes in relative income shares. These data (shown in Table 6.6) basically confirm the earlier picture: the middle-income group gained most during the 1961–71 decade, while the poorer groups gained less, and the poorest 10 per cent gained a mere 1 per cent annually. These estimates are based on real per capita income growth. In failing to realise any significant gains in real income, the poorest decile actually lost ground in terms of relative income shares. In contrast with the static picture shown in Tables 6.4 and 6.5, the shifts in the 1961–71 period were more favourable to the middle group (20–80 percentiles) and less favourable to the richest (80–100). It should be remembered, however, that the reduced rate of income growth for the rich still meant greater absolute income gains than those achieved by the poor. In other words, the absolute gap in incomes was increasing not only between the poor and middle income groups, but between the lower and upper ends of the middle range. The very poor, occupying the lowest decile, faced not only a widening gap in absolute terms and a loss of

TABLE 6.6   Growth in real household income by decile, Costa Rica
1961–71

Income percentile	Share of house-hold income 1961	Share of house-hold income 1971	Changes, 1961—71 Percentage point change in relative income shares	Changes, 1961—71 Average annual rate of growth of incomes
	(1) %	(2) %	(3)	(4) %
Poorest 0–10	2.6	2.1	−0.5	0.9
10–20	3.1	3.3	0.2	3.8
20–30	3.3	4.1	0.8	5.3
30–40	4.0	5.1	1.1	5.7
40–50	4.8	6.2	1.4	5.8
50–60	5.9	7.6	1.7	5.8
60–70	7.6	9.4	1.8	5.4
70–80	10.1	11.8	1.7	4.7
80–90	14.6	16.2	1.6	4.2
90–100	44.0	34.2	−9.2	0.6
Total	100.0	100.0	0.0	3.1

SOURCES
UN, ECLA, *Economy Survey of Latin America, 1968* and Victor Hugo Cespedes S., *Costa Rica: La Distribución del Ingreso y el Consumo de Algunos Alimentos,* Universidad de Costa Rica Serie Economía y Estadística, no. 45 (San José, n.d.), as quoted in Shail Jain, *Size Distribution of Income* (Washington, DC: World Bank, 1975) p. 27. IMF, *International Financial Statistics*, May 1978.

Urban poverty and economic development

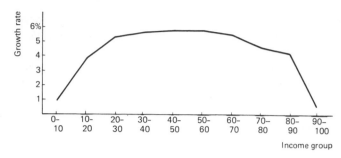

FIG. 6.2.   Average annual income growth, 1961–71 by income decile

relative share, but a stagnation in the rate of income growth itself. Figure 6.2 illustrates these relationships.

One important conclusion may be drawn from this discussion. Strategies aimed at serving the poor, generally defined as being 'below the median income level', seem likely to serve those closest to the median, that is to say, the 40–60 percentile group who were already reaping the major benefits of Costa Rican economic growth. The 20–40 group was also gaining, according to data from the 1960s: more recent policies seem to have genuinely succeeded in benefiting this group.

The real losers always have been and apparently continue to be the poorest decile. This group requires highly imaginative policy design in all areas – whether health, employment, income generation, housing, or other – in order to overcome the distinctive constraints of reaching this group. There needs to be rigorous monitoring of the target efficiency of programmes, especially in light of the extremely powerful and persistent trickle-up forces which traditionally divert programme benefits from the lowest- to the middle-income groups.

If these data are accurate, the failure of past programmes to serve the poorest has major implications both for analysing the nature of poverty in a country like Costa Rica, and for designing and monitoring policy interventions. More specifically:

(a) The analysis of poverty should take into account not only the programmes intended to serve the poor, but other social forces and institutions which despite all intentions are recreating inequalities in relative income shares.

(b) The design and monitoring of policies should be more explicit about their target efficiency, that is, their real effectiveness in serving the lowest two or three deciles, and in containing the 'trickling up' of benefits to higher income groups.

7   Social and historical approaches to poverty assessment

This chapter deals with measurement and analysis of poverty when it is conceived as a phenomenon that goes beyond a mere problem of deficient incomes. We will be dealing in this chapter with three more approaches to poverty assessment, each relating to social conditions and forces bearing on the status of the poor and their potential for change. The first deals with social indicators, particularly in regard to the infrastructure of poor communities. The second deals with access by the poor to social and economic capital that might provide leverage for development. The third addresses broader historical processes that determine opportunities or barriers to progress. Once again, the empirical observations concentrate on Costa Rica.

4 SOCIAL INDICATORS

Social indicators supplement income data in describing the livelihood and wellbeing of poor people. The two kinds of data are closely, but not perfectly correlated. In this section, we see that place of residence – whether in a city slum (*tugurio*) or not – does not seem to play a key role as an indicator of poverty. This reinforces our earlier impression that urban poverty was not a spatially delimited phenomenon. Slums in San José were not notably distinctive from other parts of the city with respect to the amounts of poverty they harboured, whether poverty was measured in terms of income or by other social characteristics.

Table 7.1 compares *tugurio* (T) and non-*tugurio* (NT) populations in the San José Metropolitan Area with regard to family size, age composition, labour force participation, and employment. As in the chapter dealing with migration, three income strata were viewed, using the 1973 census tabulations.

114

TABLE 7.1 Family size and economic activity, by neighbourhood and income level, San José Metropolitan Area, 1973

	Line	T = Tugurio NT=Non-Tugurio	All incomes by neighbourhood	All incomes area wide	Less than ¢1300 'Subsistence'	Less than ¢2000 'Poor'	Above ¢2000 'Non-Poor'
Average family size	1	T	5.57	5.31	6.55	6.49	4.78
	2	NT	5.27		6.07	6.25	4.89
Average no. of potential earners in family (ages 15-64)	3	T	2.98	3.07	2.62	2.87	3.07
	4	NT	3.09		2.61	2.87	3.17
Average no. of economically active persons in family	5	T	1.74	1.75	1.23	1.47	1.98
	6	NT	1.75		1.02	1.29	1.92
Dependency rate	7	T	0.87	0.73	1.50	1.27	0.54
	8	NT	0.70		1.32	1.17	0.54
Labour force participation rate (LFPR)	9 Men	T	90%		84%	87%	91%
	10	NT	82%		70%	76%	84%
	11 Women	T	29%		19%	22%	34%
	12	NT	34%		17%	20%	40%
	13 Both sexes	T	58%		47%	51%	63%
	14	NT	56%		39%	44%	60%
Unemployment rates	15 Men	T	9%		24%	17%	4%
	16	NT	6%		25%	16%	3%
	17 Women	T	5%		11%	9%	3%
	18	NT	2%		9%	7%	2%
	19 Both sexes	T	8%		21%	15%	4%
	20	NT	5%		21%	14%	2%
Proportion of families with per capita incomes shown	21	T	100.0	100.0	26.8%	46.3%	53.7%
	22	NT	100.0		15.3%	27.8%	72.1%

SOURCE
1973 Population Census.

115

Average family size (Table 7.1, lines 1 and 2). Poor families were bigger than other families. The poorest families in *tugurios*, averaging 6.55 members, were larger by about half a person than poorest families in other city neighbourhoods (6.07 members). Even larger differentials marked comparisons of families above and below the ₡2,000 poverty line.

Potential earners (ages 15–64) per family (lines 3–6). Larger family size was associated with greater numbers of children, not adults. The numbers of adults in *tugurio* families was almost exactly the same as the number of adults in families living elsewhere. Neither type of neighbourhood had an advantage, therefore, with respect to potential numbers of income earners. The remaining differences, while greater, were still insubstantial in regard to numbers of persons who were actually economically active, that is, who were members of the labour force.

Dependency rate (lines 7 and 8). The dependency rate measures the numbers of young (under fifteen) and old (over sixty-four) persons per 100 persons of so-called 'working age' (15–64). The higher the ratio, the lower the number of potential working adults and the higher the proportion of those who, in many societies, are economically 'dependent'. While the dependency ratio in the lowest income brackets was higher in *tugurios* than elsewhere, it was virtually the same in higher income strata.

Labour force participation rates, by sex (lines 9–14). Economic activity is defined as working or actively seeking work. The labour force is therefore composed of both employed and unemployed. While considerable controversy exists about the appropriateness of this set of internationally applied definitions, especially in low-income countries, this analysis is based on the traditional definition of economic activity.

In all income strata, the number of family members in the labour force was higher in *tugurios* than outside. As incomes grow, average numbers of participants per family grow as well. However, for the top bracket – which under no circumstances could be thought to represent more than the most modest incomes – the number of family members at work or seeking work was almost exactly the same for *tugurio* and non-*tugurio* residents.

Women's participation rates are far lower, for all incomes and in both *tugurios* and outside, than in affluent countries. Higher fertility and the absence of previous female participation tradition are both reflected here. *Tugurio* women show a higher participation rate in the lower income brackets, but with higher income (more than ₡2,000), the rate for non-*tugurio* women becomes higher.

We conclude that higher participation by *tugurio* residents results in the same incomes as in non-*tugurios*. This, in turn, reflects the lower education (and probably lower skills and productivity) of *tugurio* residents, as well as relatively poor job opportunities. More of them must participate to achieve income levels equivalent to those made outside.

Unemployment rates (lines 15–20). The unemployment rate used here is the standard one: the proportion of the labour force that actively, but unsuccessfully, sought work during the survey week. The data show clearly that unemployment rates for the urban poor were high, especially among the lowest strata of the poor. Nevertheless, holding income levels constant, unemployment rates were not notably different for *tugurio* and non-*tugurio* residents. Indeed, as close inspection of the data brings out, the unemployment rates were as likely to be higher among non-*tugurio* residents as the reverse. These generalisations seem to apply equally for men and women, although women's unemployment rates were not as high as men's.

Differences among *tugurios*: statistics and intangibles

Social statistics may tend to reduce people and communities to abstractions. Averages, if not supplemented by other data and perceptual sensitivities, can lead to the impression that, 'If you've seen one slum, you've seen them all'. People who have worked on *tugurio* problems in Costa Rica – or even visitors who supplement their archival research with actual site visits – quickly recognise the variations from one community to another. Many differences are subjectively clear but statistically elusive. Some differences have to do with the origins of the various slum areas. Attitudes by slum residents and leaders towards their own situation and their efforts at self-improvement depend a great deal on intangibles: sense of security, confidence in progress based on shared memories, willingness to take initiative and to undertake cooperative efforts, to trust outsiders, to risk energy and capital in local ventures, to care for the shared environment against crime, vandalism, indifference, injustice, and manipulation. The particular history of success and failure in past government actions or local initiatives or foreign assistance projects – all these affect the prospects of success for new development programmes.

Most of these factors are invisible to those who stake their analysis of poverty on a purely 'objective' rendering of social statistics taken at a particular point in time. It is not our purpose to suggest any specific weighting scheme for inclusion of 'intangible' factors along with statistical portraits of reality, either in descriptions of poverty, in theories about it, or in the design of appropriate interventions. In this section, however, we wish to illustrate a series of specific points about the use of subjective factors in analysing *tugurio* characteristics. First, various Costa Rican agencies have undertaken serious efforts – and in our opinion useful ones – aimed at developing typologies of *tugurios* based on a mixture of subjective and objective factors. Experience has shown that variations among *tugurios* make a difference in the design of policies suitable to the specific needs confronted in each case. Below we describe the typologies that have been developed for these purposes in Costa Rica.

Second, although the differences between *tugurio* types seem quite obvious to first-hand observers (with a few exceptions discussed below), in making inter-*tugurio* comparisons, we find the same lack of statistical discrimination that turned up earlier in comparing *tugurio* sites to the rest of the San José Metropolitan Area. The differences in objective data are simply not as marked as those inspired by more subjective impressions.

Third, much research remains to be done in bringing to light the true nature of subjective characterisations of poverty. One interpretation of the near-absence of statistical differences is that poverty is a chimera. One could argue that behind the ugliness and squalor of physical appearances, people in *tugurios* are not so badly off. It follows that they need no radical intervention by outsiders: no bulldozers or special nutrition programmes or compensatory education or community development projects. They deserve equal opportunities for jobs, like anyone else. Beyond that, the best policy calls for sensitive recognition of their own resourcefulness, and responsive provision of resources to help implement programmes of their own initiative.[1]

Another interpretation suggests that present analysis has not gone far enough in exploring objective measures to confirm true differences among *tugurios* or the distinct nature of *tugurio* problems vis-à-vis other types of poverty and other urban groups. This implies, for example, the need to develop consensual social statistics, based on convergence among judgements made by independent observers.

The small differences among *tugurios*, measured statistically, are subject to still another interpretation. One could argue that poverty is indeed a distinct and serious problem, but that statistical measures misconstrue its true nature. According to this view, poverty has to be understood in relation to a more complete model of its causes, which operate not just in the physical proximity of the *tugurio* but in the larger structure of social institutions and forces in society at large. Beyond social indicators and limited interventions in specific manifestations of poverty, this more inclusive interpretation calls for a normative and historical examination of society as a whole, extending to global economic and political relationships, as a necessary context for getting beneath poverty symptoms to the deeper-rooted processes at work. For example, critics of conventional poverty analysis assert that the concept of poverty reflects the cultural bias of researchers who accept the prevailing cultural norms of high consumption. The dream of unlimited progress, according to these critics, is illusory. Worse, it stigmatises as 'inferior' whoever happens to find themselves at the lower end of the income distribution. In this view, the problem of rich and poor stems not just from a 'culture of poverty' but equally from the insidious consequences of a 'culture of wealth'.[2] It is not our purpose to make any choice between these interpretations, but it is worth noting that the data presented below could be seen as consistent with any of these three views.

Defining a *tugurio*

The *tugurio* sample used in this study was based on *census tract boundaries*, each *tugurio* being one tract or a group of tracts. These census-based units are referred to as '*zonas*'.

The National Institute of Housing and Urbanisation (INVU) and other Costa Rican agencies sometimes use a different way of drawing *tugurio* boundaries based on 'natural' borders such as rivers, railroad tracks, proposed or existing highways, clear and stable divisions between rich and poor neighbourhoods, and other demarcations. Defined in this way, poor areas are referred to as *'nucleos'*. They are considered relatively well defined neighbourhoods, and appropriate units for poverty intervention programmes attempting to deal with communities as integrated wholes.

To keep clear the distinction between *nucleos* and *zonas*, one should note that *zona* and *nucleo* boundaries do not coincide except by happenstance, although the two types of units naturally overlap in many cases. Both *zonas* and *nucleos* oversimplify the problem of identifying locations of poverty in San José. As noted repeatedly in this study, more than three-quarters of the poor live outside well-defined *tugurios*. Based on census data, it also is clear that substantial numbers of non-poor live in *tugurios* along with poor residents.

Throughout our own study, we refer to the (census-based) *zona* rather than the ('natural boundary') *nucleo*. The *zonas* have the advantage of corresponding to census tracts which offer a wealth of ready-made comparative data.

On the other hand, *nucleos* have possible advantages in regard to programme design and implementation, because they simplify the conceptual location of poverty on maps, and represent more agglomerated targets for services delivery. Furthermore, if data had been available for *nucleos*, they may have shown sharper statistical differences from the rest of the city, because their boundaries are specifically tailored to physical and subjective impressions of current slum borders. In contrast, census tract borders (defining *zonas*) were not usually drawn with poverty issues in mind, and were generally established in an earlier period, when the spatial distribution of slums was somewhat different.

Three major types of *tugurios*

The INVU identification of areas called *tugurio zonas* reflects both subjective judgement on conditions seen in the field, and census information on socio-economic and physical indicators. Aerial photography and on-site visits were also used by the Institute in establishing *tugurio* boundaries.

In constructing a typology of poor areas, INVU used a wide variety of measures, some straightforward, others impressionistic, some bearing on the severity of poverty, others simply describing differences in contextual conditions. *Physical* descriptions included such characteristics as deteriorated housing, lack of sanitary facilities, and crowding. *Economic* factors included rough estimates of unemployment, income and wealth (based on an inventory of possessions), and – very important – the status of land tenancy. This referred not only to renting and ownership but also to the status of land occupied, whether held in private or public hands, whether under formal or informal terms of occupancy, and whether there appeared long- or short-term prospects for stable assurance of continued uses. *Social* factors included levels of education and literacy. Other subjective impressions were also incorporated into the INVU typology, such as *rural features* (scarcity of infrastructure, plots for small scale cultivation, lifestyles different from urban norms).

In 1977, staff from the National Planning Office took the INVU typologies and data on *tugurios* and constructed their own more simplified typology, broken down into three major types.

Type I: Concentrated ('circunscrito' or 'continuo'). Tugurios in large, continuous, and clearly bounded zones, easily recognisable. Generally formed in the period immediately after World War II. 1973 population: about 16,000, which was 22 per cent of the *tugurio* population and 3 per cent of the total San José Metropolitan Area.

Type II: Dispersed ('diseminado'). Poverty and poor housing mixed with higher-standard units. Of more recent formation, and attributed largely to influx of migrants during the 1960s. 1973 population: about 30,000 or 41 per cent of the *tugurios* and 6 per cent of the San José Metropolitan Area.

Type III: Unstable pockets ('focalizado'). Generally small and isolated groups of diverse age and origin, clearly demarked in strips and pockets, sometimes the result of organised groups of squatters ('invasions'). They are relatively unstable. 1973 population: 27,000 or 36 per cent of the *tugurio* population and 5 per cent of San José. Two-thirds of this population was located on private land, and one-third on municipal land.

As emphasised above, statistical measures of differences in socio-economic characteristics of these three groups are not very marked. Some variations can, however, be detected suggesting the possible need for differential treatment as targets of poverty intervention policies.

Type I Tugurios: concentrated

Concentrated older city slums make up the smallest proportion of the total *tugurio* population – a fact which in itself is interesting since these concentrations represent the usual stereotype of urban slums. Moreover, as the dominant poverty stereotype, concentrated *tugurios* tend to be the principal objective of public policy.

This point is specially relevant because other types of *tugurios*, though not as large or visibly knitted together, may have cohesive elements not well captured by any description which gives special emphasis to physical appearances. In contrast, concentrated *tugurios* offer relatively well defined targets for delivery of poverty intervention programmes, and therefore pose better possibilities of coordination among agencies around needs of specific zones.

Theory and evidence from studies made in other Latin American cities show that cohesive slum areas, far from being a problem, serve actually as a solution to many of the basic needs of low-income people.[3] It has been shown elsewhere that well-established shanty towns offer a micro-society of opportunities for upward mobility; they tend to be self-policing; the shelter, though unappealing by middle-class standards, tends to reflect rational economic choice in terms of the amount of investment affordable and the kinds of raw materials used. As a consequence, this type of concentrated *tugurio*, which may be the most viable and 'rational' form of urban poverty, is precisely the kind most vulnerable to extermination by eradication policies of poverty intervention. Socially organised to take advantage of their own resources, they are also easy targets for bulldozers.

Few dramatic differences separated concentrated (Type I) *tugurios* from the other two types (see Table 7.2), but the following points were notable:

(i) Labour participation rates were slightly lower for men and higher for women, compared to Types II and III *tugurios* (see rows 7 and 9 of Table 7.2).
(ii) Slightly more family heads worked in the tertiary (services) sector and fewer in the secondary (manufacturing) sector (rows 11, 12).
(iii) A greater percentage of the houses owned by residents were in 'bad' condition (row 20).
(iv) A significantly lower proportion of houses were owned by residents, possibly owing to the more established character of the

TABLE 7.2 Socio-economic characteristics of three *tugurio* types

	Total Metropolitan Area	Non-tugurio metropolitan areas	Total tugurios	Type I concentrated	Type II dispersed	Type III: unstable pockets On municipal land	Type III: unstable pockets On private land
1 No. of families	94,442	81,203	13,239	3,148	5,134	1,663	3,294
2 No. of individuals	501,316	427,566	73,750	16,547	30,211	9,348	17,644
3 Percentage of families with 8 or more persons	18	18	23	20	26	24	20
4 Percentage of family heads 45 years or older	43	44	38	41	36	38	39
5 Median family income (₡)	20,512	21,686	13,313	13,068	12,311	14,716	14,403
6 Median per capita income (₡)	3,082	3,300	2,140	2,317	1,848	2,358	2,430
7 Labour participation–males	83%	82%	90%	87%	92%	89%	88%
8 Unemployment–males	7%	6%	9%	9%	11%	9%	8%
9 Labour participation–females	34%	34%	29%	31%	25%	31%	31%
10 Unemployment–females	2%	2%	5%	5%	6%	6%	3%
11 Percentage of family heads in secondary economic sector	25	24	32	28	33	31	33
12 Percentage of family heads in tertiary economic sector	52	53	46	50	42	48	47

(contd)

TABLE 7.2 Socio-economic characteristics of three *tuguario* types (*contd*)

	Total Metro-politan Area	Non-tuguario metro-politan areas	Total tugurios	Type I concen-trated	Type II dispersed	Type III: unstable pockets On munici-pal land	On private land
13 Percentage of family heads with no formal education	5	4	8	7	10	7	8
14 Percentage of economically active males with no formal education	2	2	4	3	6	4	4
15 Percentage of economically active females with some primary education	18	18	20	20	19	21	21
16 Percentage of persons with incomes < ₡1300/year	20	–	32	28	38	26	
17 Percentage of persons with incomes > ₡2000/year	64	–	46	50	38	53	
18 Percentage of families who who are migrants	18	–	21	10	30	18	
19 Percentage of houses owned (not rented)	58	–	50	35	61	48	
20 Percentage of owned houses in 'bad' condition	14	–	31	35	27	33	

SOURCE
1973 Census.

124

economic infrastructure in Type I *tugurios* (which were oldest), and the greater specialisation of economic functions in such areas.
(v) *A very low percentage of families were urban migrants.* The figure of 10 per cent is far below that of Types II and III *tugurios*, and far below the San José average (18 per cent).

The last finding reflects the established nature of Type I (concentrated) *tugurios*, and further indicates that there was a relatively low rate of population turnover within such areas. Such areas were neither attractive nor expulsive in character, but stable. In short, their inhabitants were 'loyal to home', if voting with one's feet means anything.

Type II Tugurios: dispersed

The more recent formation of these areas may explain some of their distinctive socio-economic characteristics, although only a few of these are noteworthy.

(i) Residents were somewhat poorer on average than those in Types I and III *tugurios* (rows 5, 6).
(ii) Family size was somewhat larger (row 3).
(iii) Male labour force participation rates were high and female rates were low, an exaggeration of the way that *tugurios* generally differ from non-*tugurio* areas (rows 7, 9).

Type III Tugurios: unstable pockets

Not much distinguishes these *tugurios* generically from the other two types, probably because the typology represents a residential mix of differing poverty circumstances not clearly falling into the other two categories. Whereas Types I and II were associated with particular historical periods (the post-war and the 'sixties), these represented a more varied set of origins. For some measurements, Type III *tugurios* were split between those located on private land and those on publically owned land. The distinction affects what can can or should be done in these neighbourhoods, but otherwise there was little discernible difference between them, or between the generic Type III and the average *tugurio* experience elsewhere.

The one notable feature of Type III *tugurios* was their slight advantage with respect to income levels, which were higher here than the *tugurio* average. However, incomes were still well below other San José areas, although the other non-*tugurio* areas of San José contain a substantial majority of the city's poor.

Conclusions on social indicators of poverty

The data reviewed above suggest that poverty only loosely corresponds to geographical zones. Poor people cannot be identified very well by their spatial location. Poverty is a condition that permeates the whole urban field almost to the same degree as it dwells in visible slums.

Such a finding is somewhat counter-intuitive. One can traverse the city of San José by foot, car or plane, and easily distinguish between shanties and mansions, between houses with car-ports and crowded tenements, between urchins playing barefoot in the dust and young people in tennis whites at the country club. The data tell us, however, that each neighbourhood is more diverse than the dominant image that commands our eyes' attention. In our visual thinking, we tend to be holistic and synthetic.[4] We superimpose graphic, inclusive symbols of wealth or poverty upon an entire area, ascribing intelligible character to a physical entity, and synthesising the disparate parts into a simpler, more coherent mental picture.

The objective data, on the other hand, call attention to the range of incomes and ways of life that mingle within a particular urban space. Calling the space a 'neighbourhood' suggests the existence of social networks and shared activities that connote homogeneous class groupings. In contrast, if we take a census within physically determined boundaries, we uncover a significant number of persons who do not belong to our impressionistic stereotypes. Squatters turn up in odd corners of upper class suburbs, while prosperous merchants, off-beat professionals, and tenacious property owners make decent quarters in otherwise dilapidated zones shunned by the more status-conscious social climbers of the middle class.

Both subjective impressions and objective data might guide the exploration of poverty in San José. The disparity between impressions and data has several implications for the conduct of poverty investigation. We point out three here. First, appearances can deceive. The visual manifestations of poverty – or wealth, for that matter – are partly superficial. Physical appearances may be accurate indicators of genuine problems, but they can also lead to an over-simplified image of particular neighbourhoods. The apparent problems may not be shared by all or even most of the district's inhabitants.

Perceiving a neighbourhood as a unitary phenomenon has dangers for policy prescription as well as for analysis. If we see an area with shacks, sick children, and visible unemployment, then we may be tempted to apply area-wide solutions that could help only a few, and even harm others. Or our policies might serve those who are already well off, whose presence we overlooked, but who tend to be in the best position to take advantage of new jobs or houses or credit arrangements or training opportunities. At the same time, one might pass over wealthy neighbourhoods without second thought to the serious needs of poverty enclaves that may exist within them.

In short, poverty strategies need to be directed to individuals and families or to cooperative organisations that need assistance and can use the particular kind being offered. Assistance aimed at physical entities, on the other hand, can squander public funds on unfocused solutions.

A second implication drawn from our study of poverty indicators in San José is the need for procedures to create a systematic confrontation between quantitative data and visual impressions. We have alluded to the marked disparity between these two sources. This may reflect data error or observer bias that could be corrected by exposure to evidence derived in different fashion. But perhaps no error is involved. Each method of investigation tends to focus on a different, though genuine, aspect of poverty. A particular neighbourhood, while composed of very disparate groups, also has coherent aspects, beginning with its physical boundaries. Its residents are all affected by each other's behaviour, served by the same political representatives, touched by the same local events, and sometimes educated in the same schools.

A final conclusion relates to the general question of social indicators for poverty and the appropriate form of statistical analysis. The data just presented for San José are fairly detailed and deliberately oriented to the specific task of measuring poverty, both in delineating differentiated poverty neighbourhoods (Type I, II, and III *tugurios*) and in selective comparison of poverty thresholds (the ₡1,300 and ₡2,000 income levels). Consequently the data should be reasonably adequate as a guide for locating poverty groups, and are clearly superior to the information usually on hand to guide policy design for specific urban areas.

Had the study used more sophisticated techniques of statistical analysis, it might have established stronger correlations between the physical entity of *tugurios* and the social indicators of poverty. Yet there are practical limits to the use of more complicated analytical procedures. In most cities, data are not regularly collected that would feed this kind of analysis. *Ad hoc* studies done for one site or one date might not be valid for others. Government agencies, in any case, rarely pore over elaborate quantitative analysis in determining priorities or designing poverty intervention programmes.

Finally, as one begins to take a closer, more refined analytical look at poverty in specific sites, the concept of poverty as a general condition tends to break down and give way to concrete issues, such as health, shelter, jobs, education, and other basic needs. Especially important, one has to begin looking at attitudes toward change and institutional means for attacking the problems of poverty. These matters are addressed in the next section.

5 ACCESS TO CAPITAL. ORGANISATIONAL INFRASTRUCTURE

Access to capital sensitively measures the potential for poor people to improve their situation through social and economic leverage on their environment. Here the analysis shifts from a static picture of poverty conditions as they are or were, to a stronger focus on ways people can control their own futures.

As mentioned earlier, capital may refer to *economic* assets (credit, land, education), or to *social* assets. The latter take the form of organisations, social movements, political networks, managerial talent, and other factors which provide a fulcrum for economic levers of progress. In this section, we concentrate mainly on 'social capital', in part because it happens that such data are more readily available in Costa Rica, and in part because these are less often recognised as elements of poverty intervention strategies. Chapter 8 comments on access to sources of finance for housing.

Tugurio organisations

Information on Costa Rican *tugurio* organisations was available from three principal sources: DINADECO (The National Agency for Community Development), IMAS (The Social Assistance Institute) and the household survey carried out by the National Office of Information in 1977.

Table 7.3 indicates that no single form of community organisation attracted the active participation of more than 10 per cent of *tugurio* inhabitants. Education groups were most important in this respect, followed by community development associations, political parties, labour unions, church groups, and cooperatives. Municipality associated groups generated lesser numbers of participants than nutrition center committees.

In most cases, the participation rate was on the order of 5 per cent. It did not vary notably among the different types of organisations and sectoral concerns shown in Table 7.3. Five per cent may not appear very high, but it is necessary to keep in mind

TABLE 7.3   Participation in community meetings among residents of *tugurios* in the San José Metropolitan Area

Communal and local government organis- ations	Attendance rates			*Not attend- ding*	*Total respon- dents*	*Rank*
	Mem- bers %	*Non- mem- bers* %	*Total* %	%	%	
Municipality	1.0	3.3	4.3	95.7	100.0	7
School board	1.7	7.4	9.1	90.9	100.0	1
Community Develop- ment Association	2.0	4.1	6.1	93.9	100.0	2
Nutrition Center Committee	0.6	1.4	2.0	98.0	100.0	8
Cooperative	2.1	3.0	5.1	94.9	100.0	6
Church Board	2.2	3.1	5.3	94.7	100.0	5
A political party	2.4	3.3	5.7	94.3	100.0	3
A labour union	3.1	2.5	5.6	94.4	100.0	4
Other	3.3	5.0	8.3	91.7	100.0	–

SOURCE
OFIPLAN survey, 1977.

that:

(a) Different people belonged to different organisations, so the total participation rate was considerably higher.

(b) Responses probably referred to continuous participation, but on a short-term basis, for purposes of seeking action on specific issues, the number of people involved may be higher than shown.

(c) The rate probably varied from one *tugurio* to the next both in overall rate of participation and in relative strength of different types of organisations. Rates probably also varied within *tugurios*, from one block to the next, and from one time to another, depending on particular needs and local events.

(d) A 5 per cent rate of active participation is perhaps not low compared with other groups in Costa Rica, or *tugurio*-based populations in other countries (but no data are presently available on this).

(e) The intensity of participation varied from one type of organisation to the next. For example, 'attendance' is high in education, but 'membership' low, while the reverse is true for labour unions. The quality of 'membership' also undoubtedly varied, calling upon different degrees of commitment and hours spent and initiative called for, depending on the type of organisation.

Table 7.4 turns attention from the question of continuous participation in specific organisations to the question of which channels *tugurio* residents would use for action on *ad hoc* or general grievances.[5] About a third would rely on existing local government (municipality – 11 per cent; Community Development Association – 21 per cent); another segment would use political channels (congressional representative – 19 per cent, political party channels – 4 per cent); while another third would use *ad hoc* arrangements (organising meetings with neighbours – 28 per cent, organising strikes – 3 per cent). There is a small category of unspecified measures that people would take (14 per cent), but only 3.5 per cent of the sample of 517 adults said they would do nothing. In real situations people might act differently than shown in their response to the hypothetical survey question, but there was very little overt cynicism or indifference in these returns, given the mere 3.5 per cent of 'do nothing' responses.

Costa Rica's social and political analysts have also commented upon the political role of such community based organisations and

TABLE 7.4   *Tugurio* residents' opinions on effective mechanisms for con-
fronting Government agencies with local problems

Mechanisms	Number	Percentage
Established institutions		
Municipality	57	11
Community Development Association	109	21
		32
Political channels		
Congressional representative (*diputado*)	98	19
Political party representative	18	3
		22
Ad hoc measures		
Organise meetings with neighbours	146	28
Organise a strike	18	3
		31
Other	53	10
Do nothing	18	3
Total sample (adults)	517	100

SOURCE
OFIPLAN survey, 1977.

their relationships with official support systems. They point out
that the government works at different levels of formal and
informal support to maintain influence over these neighbourhoods.
It establishes the greatest possible number of intermediaries, and
thus diffuses power. It also supplies a complicated network of
concessions to local leaders, who are concerned about their own
personal interests and consequently minimise conflict with or
questioning of the political machinery. A scheme of mutual
manipulation is established in which the Government or other
established source of power supplies the necessary aid and
protection against legal and illegal activities of authority, while the
client responds with demonstrations of confidence, information
about the activities of other groups, and political support. In this
way, the state apparatus avoids conflicts and manifestations of
violence through mechanisms of negotiation and transaction, thus
influencing the communal and political attitudes of poor persons.

Some evidence and local testimony about Costa Rican *tugurios* suggest they are more organised and capable of mobilising themselves for collective action than might be perceived by inventories of established agencies operating on their behalf. The first mechanism that *tugurio* people rely upon is meetings with neighbours (28 per cent of responses in Table 7.4), followed by working through Community Development Association (21 per cent). This indicates a tendency toward self-reliance, and/or distrust of traditional mechanisms. For example, note the relatively low use of municipal channels. It has also been observed by people who have worked in *tugurio* areas that residents spontaneously organise themselves into pressure groups for purposes of getting immediate action on well focused problems, for example, securing rights to land when residents are subject to expulsion. Once the objective has been met, the group often dissolves. This does not conform to the usual bureaucratic view of an effective organisation, and this makes it hard for traditional service agencies to deal with them. Nevertheless, *tugurio* residents are perhaps wise in avoiding bureaucratic methods and standards of efficiency in dealing with the kind of problems they face. Their willingness to organise, however, does provide opportunities to develop meaningful community development programmes, based upon local desires and implemented by local talent.

6 POVERTY IN HISTORICAL PERSPECTIVE

Up to this point, we have focused on poverty conditions within a fairly short time frame, encompassing the immediate past and the near future. Now we turn to a longer perspective, and a more value-explicit treatment of poverty.

The historical perspective is perhaps an obvious point of departure for analysis of large scale social processes and problems. The present book, for example, introduced Costa Rica through an initial exposition of major historical forces operating on the spatial distribution of population and economic activities in that country. Nevertheless, typical documents on poverty assessment or urban and regional analysis introduce historical commentary only to set the stage for subsequent methodological treatments which are themselves largely devoid of reference to long-term evolution of complex relationships of social transformation. Analysts seem to recognise the importance of historical processes but once having cited history as prefatory background, they proceed to more conventional methods of social science which make no provision for incorporation of historical insights. In short, history is typically accorded a role in making ceremonial introductions, but not in constituting an analytical tool in its own right.

Some of the strengths and limitations of historical analysis have been mentioned earlier, in comparing this approach with more conventional treatments of poverty. Briefly, we believe that the other five approaches discussed earlier are empty without an understanding of the historical evolution of social institutions that led to the conditions of poverty being measured. Most concepts and measures of poverty focus narrowly on problems rather than the circumstances which created them or continue to sustain them. Most analyses deal with a limited time frame of current ills and near-future solutions, ignoring the deeper processes of social transformation which can only be seen on a scale of decades. In the short run, historical circumstances that affect the depth and breadth of poverty in any particular society appear as fixed and inflexible. Policies can only nibble at the edge of underlying causes and conditions, giving most help to people already poised to take most advantage of new opportunities. From a longer-range perspective, however, the environment appears more malleable. The circumstances of wealth and poverty are more visibly products of historical processes that are themselves manmade.

Public agencies find it difficult to apply the historical approach owing to its *normative content*. Historical analysis is necessarily interpretive, and interpretation is always premised, explicitly or implicitly, on value-based norms. Norms for interpreting history may refer to optimism or pessimism about human nature, leading to biases of faith alternatively favouring the masses, the successful, the elites, the well-educated foreign advisors, or other groups. Norms may refer to the stability or instability of social institutions, depending on how the analyst views the record of past events. Norms dictate the inclusion or exclusion of the 'relevant' data in defining standards for measuring advancement of poor groups. Norms influence the interpretation of causality, for example in explaining processes variously as the result of traditional systems, or upstart pressure groups, or recourse to violence.

One of the more familiar normative historical interpretations of poverty is Marxism. The Marxist approach has certain features which we think are important for any historical treatment of poverty issues. It outlines explicitly the normative premises underlying the analysis. It refers to social institutions which determine the distribution of wealth and power. It emphasises processes of change, particularly in looking at transformation in social institutions as a product of complex conditions and forces operating throughout society in its entirety. These useful elements of historical analysis can be clearly appreciated without the need to embrace the whole Marxist theory as a package. The Marxist theory of class struggle, the specific Marxist model of revolutionary transformation, and the prediction of a victorious proletarian dictatorship are not central to our exposition. We do see, however, the need for alternative interpretations of poverty in broad normative and historical terms, focusing particularly on processes of development and transformation of social institutions.

• Examples of normative historical approaches to urban analysis can be found in non-Marxist literature: Lewis Mumford's *The City in History* and *The Pentagon of Power*, Jane Jacobs' *The Death and Life of Great American Cities*, and Ebenezer Howard's *Garden Cities of Tomorrow*.[6] The mainstream literature in urban and regional planning, however, is basically ahistorical in its focus and method. A brief description of this tradition makes clear the shortcomings and opportunities for historical analysis in this field.

Conventional urban and regional planning

In industrialised countries and elsewhere, questions of economic policy are frequently raised in a spatial context. Whether concerned with migration and settlement, depressed area economies, urban labour absorption, the location of economic activities, or rural poverty, planners are called upon to identify and analyse these problems and to suggest policies and implement measures for meeting them. The prime locus of intervention may be national, regional or local. Often, policy requires the coordination of efforts at all three levels.

The field of urban-regional policy studies is rich in hypotheses, insights, and analytical methods. In its eclectic multidisciplinarity, no general model has emerged. Urban and regional economics, location economics, and human resource economics are recognised subdisciplines within the field of economics; geography has evolved its own analytical modes to study such questions as innovation diffusion, urban hierarchies, and spatial organisation; and the synthetic field of regional science represents an attempt to introduce spatial variables explicitly into policy analysis.

Urban analysis may be considered a special case of regional analysis, in that urban patterns are often derived from processes generated elsewhere. For example, urban squatter settlements may result from expulsive forces operating in the countryside – drought, for example, or agricultural modernisation. Traffic congestion may result from the influence of automobile marketing, or foreign technical assistance emphasising roadbuilding over other forms of public transit, or housing policies promoting suburbanisation with the consequent longer journey to work.

One specialised branch of planning deals with urban systems, concerned with the size, location, and functions of all urban centres within a region. The urban system is viewed as an interconnected set of nodes for the provision of needed urban functions. Owing to economies of scale and locational advantages, cities specialise in the functions they provide. For example, large metropolitan areas may concentrate in activities such as national or regional government, international marketing, export industries, higher education, industrial agglomerations linked by the need for face-to-face interaction, communication and transportation centres, financial headquarters, or specialised medicine. Small rural service towns have other characteristic functions: marketing for agricultural products, unspecialised commercial activity, provision of basic social services such as health care, education and local government, and possibly food processing industries linked to local agriculture. In general, urban analysis identifies regions which are lacking key urban functions, or cities with similar deficiencies. This is often referred to as 'urban functional analysis'.

One function of cities and regions is to serve as loci for employment and income. Questions of poverty are often addressed in terms of economic activity that will absorb the poor. Familiar strategies include public works investments, provision of social amenities to rural towns in an effort to slow urban migration, and subsidies to encourage decentralisation of industry to poorer peripheral regions outside metropolitan centres. All over the world – in France, Brazil, England, Venezuela, United States of America, Saudi Arabia, and other countries – whole cities have been designed and constructed as 'growth poles' to spur the development of peripheral regions.

Trends in urban and regional analysis

During the 1970s, many of the traditions and underlying assumptions of urban and regional planning came under criticism. Much of the work seemed unrelated to policy. People might be able to design cities on paper, or rearrange them on maps, but political execution and control over individuals' locational preferences proved another matter. For example, improvement of rural schools will not make farm work appear more attractive; on the contrary, amenities brought to the countryside almost inevitably reflect the biases of an urban culture, stimulating movement towards the cities. Similarly, investors have frequently proven resistant to government incentives for industry to locate in provincial areas.

Some of the recent criticism has focused on the naïveté of planners – the abstraction of their economic models, and the oversimplifications made in describing functions served by cities and regions. In particular, critics have cited the neglect of market mechanisms, the failure to appraise realistically the motives underlying behaviour of individuals and firms as a basis for explaining the nature and location of economic activities, and the failures of public policy in trying to override the 'natural' course of economic development.[7]

In light of the shortcomings of traditional analysis, there seems to be increasing recognition of the value of historical approaches. Greater attention is being given to historical cases of departures from the norm, rather than purely descriptive analysis of past experience, or search for internationally typical patterns, or detailed calculations of the scope of problems at any given moment in a particular place. Less emphasis is put on measuring gaps, and more on identifying mechanisms that create or narrow the gaps. This explains in part the current interest in China, for its apparent success in radically transforming widespread conditions of poverty in the course of a few decades, at the same time preserving historical traditions that have served to maintain an integrity of rural and urban functions, through design of cultural institutions, economic activities, and spatial planning.

Learning from other countries' success has provided one motive for injection of historical analysis into urban and regional planning. Another, probably more powerful motive is the growing awareness of need to learn from our own past failures. The 'trickle down' effect providing the foundation of conventional development strategies no longer has the same credibility it used to. Major objectives for alleviating poverty in the 1960s proved unattainable without far more fundamental changes in national policies to reach marginal populations. Based on accumulating evidence of the post-World War II period, many saw increasing tendencies towards unequal, polarised development, with past strategies helping the modern sector in the metropolitan economy, and harming those already lagging behind in consolidating themselves into the international stereotype of industrial development.[8]

Few theories have been well articulated that describe the problems of poverty or opportunities for intervention in broad historical terms. Many existing models have been dismissed as ideologically suspect (Marx) or unrealistically utopian (Ebenezer Howard's *Garden Cities of Tomorrow*, already cited), or John Friedmann's work on agropolitan development,[9] or conceptually and empirically flawed (the Club of Rome's work on limits to growth), or politically naïve (various efforts towards self-sufficient, low-technology development). Some approaches used to gain broad understanding of issues – the 'systems approach' or 'ecological perspective' – are fairly watered down in most practical applications, both in respect to normative content and rigorous historical method.

Another difficulty dogs the application of historical models to problems of poverty. Most development agencies – international development banks, technical assistance organisations, consulting groups – find it hard to use the larger historical perspective in fulfilling short-term task-oriented missions. Their employees feel that they cannot affect the larger historical variables. They lack time to reflect on the implications of historical processes for their personal roles and goals. They often face conflicts between their short-run objectives – for example, more housing now – and their longer term goals, such as laboriously teaching people to build their own houses. Much if not most historical interpretations require such large amounts of faith, risk-taking, commitment, and ideology that functionaries in big public organisations are made uncomfortable by the prospect.

Costa Rica faces the same problems as any other country in applying historical analysis to the task of urban analysis. In some respects, the prospects there are better than for most other countries. The approach requires a broad political imagination, a clearly articulated concept of social justice, a willingness to intervene in economic and social structure (at comparable economic and social cost), the power to inspire public support for long-range objectives, and flexibility in public agencies to respond to macro-level demands for coordination on the one hand, and micro-level (community and individual) demands for sensitivity to local needs and wants on the other. In many of these respects, Costa Rica appears well advanced, by any standard.

Costa Rica: application of the historical approach

Major historical forces shaping the distribution of population, economic activity and poverty in Costa Rica have already been described in Chapter 2. We outlined there the historical tendency towards spatial decentralisation away from San José prior to World War II; reversal of the trend in the decades following, and the increasingly pronounced suburbanisation in the 1960s, with highest growth in the outer belt of the San José urban agglomeration, and an actual loss of population in the central city of San José itself. The historical forces affecting these shifts were described, as well as policy successes and failures in trying to counteract 'natural' trends which had resulted in problems of unplanned growth and lost economic opportunities for the poor.

The purpose of the present discussion is not to elaborate on that earlier chapter, but to describe the general scope of historical analysis as one of six approaches to urban poverty assessment. We will conclude this section with two brief comments about appropriate further steps that historical analysis might take in the particular context of Costa Rica.

First, there are aspects of poverty that are not well presented in looking at statistical presentations of aggregate phenomena occurring in a large spatial landscape. At some point, it is necessary to focus on selected issues, to provide both needed detail and qualitative sophistication. For example, there are issues of urban poverty that revolve around questions of the quality of urban life involving other groups besides the poor. Urban transportation systems are almost always designed to accommodate private automobiles, owned more by the rich than the poor. Commercial activities and manufacturing job opportunities follow the highways built for cars, creating new opportunities for those who can drive, but removing them from those who cannot. Rising land values in the periphery benefit those with the capital to speculate early, while raising the effective cost of land, housing and living for those who are less economically competitive. The number of middlemen between farm production and central market grows with the encroachment of urban land on nearby farms, increasing the length of the food distribution chain.

Second, historical analysis has a major role to play in selectively identifying case studies of successful anti-poverty strategies in the past. Costa Rica has a fairly long history of progressive experimentation with programmes aimed at helping the poor. A notable example is the work of the Institute of Lands and Settlements (ITCO).

ITCO's experience probably has more to teach than any conventional analysis attempting to describe the issues of rural–urban spatial relationships, because ITCO has gone well beyond investigating and talking. Lessons of ITCO experience might also have something to offer in the design of viable *urban* communities for poor populations within San José. This applies particularly to methods of coordinating a diversity of support services on behalf of a well-defined territorial unit. Tactics of technical assistance, reinterpretation of existing laws for land reform, seasonal shifts of labour between private business and public or cooperative enterprise and direct marketing of farm goods between grower and consumer are examples of rural development experience that would apply to an integrated strategy of development for *tugurios* or other poor communities in the San José area. Present policies are notoriously fragmented, rarely developed with respect to poor communities as functional units, and often geared to social mobility of individuals without regard to the larger, and often negative, effects of individual mobility on the community left behind.

The chapter which follows addresses this general problem of planning and coordination among diverse agencies, whose joint efforts are clearly needed for making effective inroads on the complex problems of urban poverty.

8 Urban planning, finance, and administration

Urban and regional planning in Costa Rica, as in most other low-income countries, is not highly developed. Nevertheless, the advocates of planning are numerous and eloquent. The desire to replace 'disorder' by 'coordination' – rational, systematic, and 'scientific' – has the same appeal in Central America as it does in Europe and other industrialised countries. In the United States, for example, organisational manifestations of these sentiments are found in land use planning boards, coastal commissions, and other regulatory agencies.

In Costa Rica, many people are convinced of the potential benefits of urban and regional planning. Less clear, perhaps, are ready-made solutions to the problems – or even recognition of these problems – that are likely to accompany an urban and regional planning framework. As we have tried to emphasise throughout, the problems are multifaceted, involving conceptual difficulties, financing shortfalls, organisational gaps and duplications, and administrative frustrations. The ideological and practical distance between the cartographic draughtsman, colouring his maps in the planning office in the nation's capital, and the ultimate beneficiaries of regional policy, is greater than most planners are willing to contemplate.

Certain themes present in Latin America influence the context of Costa Rican urban policy planning. The decline of municipalities as centres of political influence and their impoverished situation of public finance is one. The creation of specialised public agencies as champions of generalised municipal development partially offsets these tendencies towards decline. The specialised agencies, however, are centrally controlled, and represent an avenue by which money can be channelled back to the municipalities without turning over to them control of the process, which remains centralised. Administrative centralisation, in turn, is as old as Spanish colonial government itself, but reflects modern influences as well. In part, the decline in the costs of information resulting from advances in electronic data processing has reinforced the worldwide tendencies toward centralisation in administration. In this way, centuries old institutional modes of behaviour are given renewed life.

Another venerable Latin American theme deals with the desirability of grass roots participation. Urban anthropologists, among others, base policy prescriptions on detailed household interviewing. They distrust, and properly so, calls for action that have evolved without contact with the poor. Another example is provided by the Roman Catholic clergy in Latin America which is riven by differences between its conservative and liberal (or even radical) elements. The latter base their views not only on a set of theological interpretations, but on their day-to-day contact with poor parishioners as well. The counter-tendencies come from educated elites, sometimes foreign, sometimes native, for whom contact with the poor is effectively shunned for reasons so profoundly psychological that we hesitate to try to explain them in these pages.

A third theme, classic in its Latin American manifestations, is the proliferation of semi-autonomous agencies as competitors to the influence and fiscal strength of central government. These agencies are 'semi-' autonomous in that they were founded by actions of the government, they share with central government the absence of profit-oriented goals, they seek instead to serve social ends, they are recognised as institutions outside the control of a given ministry, and they keep their own accounts separate from other public entities. The Costa Rican variants of this institutional arrangement are described in detail below for illustrative purposes. The detail should not obscure the general pattern. Readers familiar with other Latin American countries (and probably other low-income countries in general) will be able to identify analogous organisations in other parts of the world.

A fourth theme deals with issues of foreign technical assistance and its seeming competition with national initiatives. Local agencies are pushed by international agencies into postures and activities that they would avoid if they could direct their own affairs with complete spontaneity. They perform studies 'in order to please Washington' and use scarce resources in the process, in order to qualify for grants or loans they would otherwise lose.

A fifth theme is similar in concept, but operates at a different scale. Even in the smallest countries, questions arise about whether to maintain internal cultural differentiation, with its higher administrative costs, rather than imposing centrally directed uniformity on regional policies. Local cultural customs, so dear to folklorists, appeal to the imagination of outsiders at the same time as they stand in the way of (what passes for) modernisation.

In the chapter to follow, we survey some of the activities surrounding urban and regional planning in Costa Rica. These can be described quite briefly, since planning activities at the time of writing are still embryonic. Much more fully grown, however, is a set of institutions that affects urban and regional policy, in particular with respect to the poor who are the focus of this book as a whole.

URBAN POLICY PLANNING

National urban and regional planning in Costa Rica is still at an early stage. Pronouncements have been highly general, thereby allowing for possible modification following further analysis. Most efforts have focused on establishing the infrastructure of planning itself. This is illustrated in the following statement from the National Development Plan (1978–82), comprising the section on 'Regional and Urban Development' in its entirety:

> The strategy of regional development has as its basic objective the incorporation of natural and human resources of every region of the country in the process of increase of output and reduction of existing poverty in the peripheral regions. In this way it is hoped to diminish the disequilibria which presently are found between regions and within them.
>
> Regional development is in addition a fundamental pillar for the distribution of power, the improved spatial allocation of the better benefits of development, the fight against poverty, popular participation – all goals in order to achieve a new level of life towards which the society aspires.
>
> The creation of new jobs for the present and future active population will be proposed in a way that stimulates people to remain where they are instead of migrating to urban centres in the central region where they may suffer serious privations.
>
> In addition a system of regional and sub-regional cities and

towns will be attempted which is more appropriate for the people in every region and for their requirements.

In the case of the central region the strategy for development tends to integrate the forces for improvement in the quality of life of the inhabitants and to control the physical expansion of the urban area of San José, whose growth has been produced until now in a disordered form, with damage to the natural resources.

The National System of Urban and Regional Planning, recently begun, constitutes the principal instrument for the stimulation of regional and urban planning. It ought to be strengthened.[1]

While the rest of the plan could be read with respect to the implicit spatial policies contained in its recommendations, the section cited above is the only part of the document given over directly to regional and urban development, including rural–urban migration and the (alleged) problems of hypercephalism in the capital city of San José. We conclude that concrete forms and functions of regional planning remain in their infancy. A series of good intentions has been articulated, but the toughest questions of implementation were not asked or answered by the plan's authors.

FORMULATING NATIONAL POLICIES

The underlying substantive problems of urban and regional development in Costa Rica (and San José in particular) have been described in other chapters of this book. Specific problems relating to planning as a process can be briefly summarised as follows:

(a) Administrative centralisation is as much a part of Costa Rican life as it is elsewhere in Latin America. The problem for planning lies in the inflexibility and possibly suffocating homogeneity that centralisation can bring with it.

(b) At the same time, some administrative delegation of functions to semi-autonomous agencies has occurred. These cannot readily be coordinated by the central government. While not unique, Costa Rica is far advanced in the strength and diversity of autonomous agencies.

(c) The nature and scale of urban and regional development problems have evolved beyond the capacity of existing governmental units. Spatially, the problems of San José's Metropolitan Area and the larger Urban Agglomeration bypass traditional governmental units at municipal levels, whose boundaries no longer coincide with those of the problems.

(d) The private sector's role in coordination and cooperation with regional planning has never been clear. Public sector activity such as bank credit, housing and jobs penetrate poor areas and sometimes have crowded out private enterprise. Whether these tendencies are in the interest of the people affected has not been closely examined.

(e) As elsewhere, new agencies, programmes, and services have been created without an analysis of historical success and failure in their predecessors. While study can lead to enervating delay in the worst circumstances, the process of building upon past success and avoiding demonstrated failure is more likely to occur if past examples of success and failure are clearly perceived by planners.

(f) Successful policies have to be based on facts, rather than misperceptions. In Costa Rica, doubtful applications of conventional wisdom can be found regarding housing policy (aesthetic prejudice against sites and services), transportation (failure to acknowledge self-defeating effects of urban throughway expansion, particularly its bias towards suburban interests and costs to the poor), migration (whose rates vary greatly according to the origin of reports), poverty (often conceived as a problem of visible slums, which is not the case in San José), and income and land distribution (assumed to be very egalitarian in a democratic and progressive society such as Costa Rica, but sometimes ignoring data or the unintended regressive effects of well intended policies).

The effort to set up new planning units indicates that policy makers have recognised these problems and have sought better information about urban and regional problems and better leverage to control them. Both improved analysis and administrative tools are needed. On the one hand, there is need for an analytical perspective that looks at the problems *from the standpoint of the poor*. There is increasing evidence from other countries to suggest that traditional policies tend to serve middle and upper income groups unless programmes are very explicitly directed to lower income groups, and unless results are carefully monitored. The difficulty of reaching the very poor was illustrated in Chapter 6: the lowest one or two income deciles of Costa Rica's population have not benefited equally from overall economic gains, even under a government dedicated to progressive policies.

New administrative tools will also need to be developed, partially through the realistic examination of past policies and a truly empirical diagnosis of poverty problems. This is needed to avoid reproducing the shortcomings of current programmes, but also to recognise the successes that Costa Rica has achieved in poverty intervention, and to carry these successes to a larger scale.

REGIONAL PERSPECTIVES IN POLICY-MAKING

We found it instructive to examine initiatives taken during the years 1976 and 1977 dealing with national urban and regional development policy. These seem representative, not only in a Costa Rican historical perspective, but probably in a more general Latin American one as well. Their heterogeneity of sources, agencies, sponsors, and suggested methods form a useful reminder of the variety of approaches that planners and analysts face. As the reader will note, the initiatives cited here do not generally represent implementation of substantive policies so much as the establishment of agencies, the enactment of enabling legislation, and preliminary background analysis of specific proposals. During the period we examined, some of the more important initiatives were the following:

(a) Proposal for creation of a governmental unit corresponding to the San José Urban Agglomeration[2].

(b) Proposal for a similar unit, headed by a Mayor, for the San José Metropolitan Area, published 28 August 1977 as draft legislation[3].

(c) A draft bill – the Rural Industries Bill of July 1976 – to encourage small and medium industries intended to slow migration to cities[4].

(d) Creation of six Planning Regions, essentially at the scale of provinces, but with very different boundaries drawn to capture their possibilities of internal integration and dynamic role within the larger national context. The 'Región Central', with a population of more than a million, extended beyond the Agglomeration to cover most of the Central Plateau, and embraced 80 per cent of the country's urban population, 63 per cent of the total population, and most of its industry, commercial and financial activity, including 86 per cent of industrial employment. The other five regions, predominantly rural, had populations in the 100–200,000 range.[5] Planning for at least two of the officially designated Regions (Central and Atlantic) began in 1977.

(e) Support by the government for building on the work of the Institute of Lands and Settlements (ITCO). President Oduber, in his May 1977 message before Congress, asked that ITCO be provided with 'large reserves of land in order to engender large nuclei of agricultural development, based on peasant small holders, technically endowed and efficient'.[6]

(f) Housing and family allowances, given special mention by the President in his May 1977 speech.

(g) Analysis of needs for the urban environment, focusing primarily on housing and employment problems. This was a major collaborative effort among a selected group of Costa Rican ministries and autonomous agencies, with technical assistance and funding provided by the US Agency for International Development (AID).

(h) Collaboration between the Office of Planning and AID on an 'urban sector assessment'.

(i) Comprehensive analysis of transportation problems in San José, including administrative aspects by the Ministry of Public Works and Transport with help from the World Bank.

SUBSTANCE AND COORDINATION OF MAJOR POVERTY PROGRAMMES

The Costa Rican Government has long been committed to the alleviation of urban poverty, but that commitment has assumed that the incidence of such poverty was restricted and would be adequately dealt with in a piecemeal manner by the ministrations of agencies which provided a variety of subsidies to the poor. Thus, the Social Assistance Institute (IMAS) has looked after the 'poorest of the poor' by construction of subsidised minimal housing. The National Institute for Housing and Urban Development (INVU) has created housing projected for the lower middle classes; the National Office of Community Development (DINADECO) has assisted in community organisation; the National Municipal Development Institute (IFAM) and the

National Institute for Water and Sewerage Service (SNAA) have dealt with environmental and infrastructure improvement. The mid-1970s also saw an increase in the activities of the Ministries of Labour and Health. The 'Programa de Asignaciones Familiares' (Family Allowances) has increasingly focused on the marginal areas of the San José Metropolitan Area. From these have come studies of unemployment and means of employing the poor, a community health programme directed at the poor, and a nutrition programme for children and pregnant and lactating women in schools and centres throughout the San José Metropolitan Area.

Costa Rican civil servants have recognised that they must approach the problem on two levels: first, defining and implementing policies designed to deal with poverty within a process of orderly urban growth, and second, instituting specific projects in which the imputs of hitherto independent entitics are coordinated, funded, and targeted upon priority problem areas.

Official entities with diverse responsibilities already perform many of the functions envisioned for an integrated strategy of poverty intervention. While coordination was not prominent, important steps had been taken, some in decades past. Historical landmarks in the development of planning capacity in Costa Rica include:

1954. Creation of the National Institute for Housing and Urban Development (INVU).

1968. Passage of Urban Planning Law, modified in 1972. It included provision for a National Urban Development Plan, a Zoning Plan and Regulative Plan. It also strengthened the role of the Housing Institute.

1963. Creation of the Office of Planning and Economic Policy (OFIPLAN), having responsibility for preparing the national budget and, following 1974, for developing a national planning system.

1971. Creation of the National Municipal Development Institute (IFAM). It supports the League of San José Municipalities and promotes a fusion of metropolitan area governments. Its municipal functions include both eradication and construction.

1974. Publication of *Plan Nacional de Desarrollo Urbano* (National Plan for Urban Development), a four-volume document prepared by the Housing Institute (INVU) and the Office of Planning (OFIPLAN).

1976. Creation of an official System of Urban and Regional Planning.

1977. Publication of the National Development Plan, a five-year plan for 1978–82, by the Office of Planning.

Other agencies involved in urban planning include the Casa Presidencial (eradication policies, *tugurio* programmes, urban remodelling); OPAM (problems of urban density and growth); Ministry of Public Works and Transport (MOPT) (urban transportation); and municipalities (eradication, construction, special programmes).

This array of agencies and sectoral foci provides an overall picture of the substantive ingredients of urban development planning in Costa Rica. If all proposals were approved, virtually every way of visualising the San José urban space would have its own government and planning system. Successive administrative units would unfold, starting from the city centre in concentric layers out to the very borders of the country and beyond, taking into account the Central American Common Market and transnational firms which have a very strong impact on urban development patterns. Whether this would provide an ultimate solution to the problem of coordinating programmes for people below the poverty line is not clear.

GROWTH OF THE PUBLIC SECTOR

The history of modern Costa Rica begins in 1949, in the aftermath of the Second World War, the Civil War of 1948 and the promulgation of the new constitution of 1949. The year 1950 is an appropriate landmark to trace the evolution of the public sector. In the quarter century 1950–75, public sector *employment* increased fourfold, growing at 6.4 per cent per year during the following decade 1965–75 (see Table 8.1). The 86,000 employees of this sector in 1975 comprised 15 per cent of all workers in the country; their output accounted for nearly 20 per cent of the gross domestic product.

Municipal government growth has been relatively slow and uneven, with a net increase of 57 per cent in employment for the decade 1965–75; the Central Government (mainly ministries) grew by 59 per cent in the same decade. The fastest increase came in the autonomous institutions of the public sector, whose decadel

TABLE 8.1   Public sector employment, 1950–75

Sector	*Number employed in thousands (and percentages)*					
	1950	*1955*	*1960*	*1965*	*1970*	*1975*
Central Government	15	22	24	28	31	45
(per cent)	(85)			(66)		(53)
Autonomous institutions	3	8	5	11	19	36
(per cent)	(15)			(26)		(41)
Municipalities	–	2	–	4	3	5
(per cent)	(0)			(8)		(6)
Total	17	32	29	43	54	86
(per cent)	(100)	(100)	(100)	(100)	(100)	(100)

NOTE
Figures in this table have been rounded and in some cases do not add to totals shown.

growth was 211 per cent. Its acceleration in the more recent five-year period is shown in Table 8.2.

Public employees made up 63 per cent of the service sector in Costa Rica in 1973. Growth of public service employment was rapid, rising from 48 to 63 per cent of the service sector in the five-year period 1968–73, while the public share of gross capital formation increased more slowly, from 24 to 28 per cent over the twelve-year period 1962–74. In this sense the evolution of the public sector was considerably more vigorous in the direction of providing services – and possibly acting as an employer of last resort – than it was in the role of exercising direct control over capital investment. (In 1976, capital expenditures made up 49 per cent of expenditures for the Central Government, and 49 per cent of expenditures by municipalities.) Also, it should be noted that a substantial part of the increased public sector employment consisted of teachers.

TABLE 8.2   Average annual rates of growth of employment, 1965–75

Municipal government	4.6%
Central government	4.7%
Autonomous institutions	7.7%
(Autonomous institutions, 1970–75)	13.3%

Some of the growth of autonomous institutions represents a takeover of functions formerly performed by the Central Government, just as the earlier decline of municipal and autonomous government employment in the 1955–60 period may have represented a centralisation of previously decentralised activities. The trend towards 'decentralisation' (actually towards administrative devolution rather than geographic diffusion of authority) created both problems and opportunities that will be discussed later in this chapter.

INSTITUTIONAL STRUCTURE OF THE PUBLIC SECTOR: AUTONOMY VS. COORDINATION

Costa Rica has many organisational units whose relationships with one another are often unclear regarding functions, required interactions, and lines of authority.

The Central Government consists of the ministries (92 per cent of its budget) as well as other constitutional bodies (8 per cent). The budgets of the ministries are approved by the President of the Republic and enacted into law by the Legislative Assembly; their budget execution and personnel management are subject to various other procedures and controls.

The autonomous institutions are headed by boards of directors, in many cases appointed by the Council of Government (that is, by the President of the Republic), and including no members who represent ministries or other agencies or special interests. This system rather effectively assures that coordination of effort cannot be enforced at the ministerial level. The agencies' operating budgets are adopted by their boards with the approval of the Controller General; and, in the case of investment or capital expenditures, of the Ministry of Planning (OFIPLAN). Most autonomous agencies are exempt from many or all of the administrative requirements to which the ministries are subject.

The process of 'decentralisation' however, has not been without reversals. As shown in Table 8.1, during the period 1955–60, functions were consolidated back into the Central Government and away from municipal and autonomous agencies. The case for coordinated government is not new, with the Spanish colonial system of administration seen as the epitomy of central coordination. The argument for coordination is heard repeatedly within planning and technical assistance circles, but it is well to review briefly the rationale for having given agencies their autonomy in recent years:

(a) They reflect new and progressive legislation that permits them to circumvent the traditional, often ponderous and inappropriate regulations of central government and to create new checks and balances between the judicial, executive, and legislative branches.
(b) They provide new organisational settings designed to accommodate new activities and decision procedures, with room for innovation and initiative-taking made possible by their very newness (apart from the formal structures). Part of this is accomplished through newly created linkages to other institutions.
(c) They provide professional depth of specialisation on focused problem areas.
(d) They separate governmental roles from party politics, and also provide continuity from one presidential administration to the next.
(e) In some respects, they may provide coordinative functions, by assuming responsibilities that cut across previous task divisions among traditional ministries.

THREE ASPECTS OF THE DECENTRALISATION ISSUE

It is important to separate three issues underlying the theme of 'decentralisation' in Costa Rica. One refers to devolution of authority to outlying regions. This is manifested in the OFIPLAN effort to create the six Planning Regions to replace (or supplant) traditional provincial divisions. A second issue concerns administrative delegation of functions between central government and autonomous agencies, the pros and cons of which have just been reviewed. The third issue, which is probably of most importance for an integrated and coordinated attack on urban poverty in selected areas, refers to the localisation of authority which requires devolution of effective power to mobilise and integrate political resources on the one hand with technical means on the other. Examples of units that might be strengthened in this way are municipalities, community development associations, or even special agencies created to represent the *tugurio nucleos* defined by INVU in collaboration with numerous other agencies, in connection with the housing and income generation projects.

A basic principle underlying this latter approach – the localisation of authority – asserts that effective coordination and adaptation of programme to needs can only take place if effective political and technical powers are vested in people who deal closely with the area or region in question. This was the basic idea of the Tennessee Valley Authority, and one of the guiding principles of the land grant college system in the United States. More recently Community Development Corporations (CDCs) have carried the same notion into the urban poverty scene. Although CDC successes have been mixed, they have helped to clarify what it takes to improve the effectiveness of new CDC efforts.[7]

INTERAGENCY COORDINATION IN RURAL AREAS

United States models cannot be directly imported to Costa Rica. Within the country itself, however, one prototype deserves special attention. The National Agricultural Council (Consejo Nacional Agropecuario, CAN) has established decentralised committees, known as CANcitos ('little CANs') in the rural areas. CANcitos were conceived to respond to the same problems of local programme coordination which confront the urban sector; therefore, their successes and failures bear careful scrutiny. The CANcito model is a good place to begin, not simply because the underlying logic is sensible, but because they have yielded a substantial body of practical experience which reveals some of the pitfalls of putting similar good ideas into practice in urban areas.

Costa Rica's National Agricultural Council (CAN) is responsible for the overall coordination of rural sector development activities. The Council's chairman is the Minister of Agriculture, and the other members are drawn from other government agencies, including three other ministries, two semi-autonomous agencies, and the Central Bank.

The Council's discussions have centred on plans for studies, projects, and plans submitted by the Agricultural Sector Planning Office (OPSA), a group of thirty technicians with specialties in planning, agricultural economics, agronomy, resources, meteorology, statistics, and other fields. Given the ability of the members to commit their respective institutions to action, the group decision becomes policy in the agricultural sector. When the Council approves a project it is passed on for implementation to the Technical Committee for Agricultural Sector Planning (COTEPSA), which consists of the heads of the planning departments of each sector institution. The system has been in full operation since mid-1976, and has achieved notable success with a coordinated cotton production project and some smaller research and survey activities.

The Council functions at the regional level through its regional councils, CANcitos, under the leadership of regional agricultural directors representing the Ministry of Agriculture. These CANcitos have been as yet largely ineffective, due to a variety of causes, including the fact that only the Ministry has truly regionalised operations. The Ministry has divided the country into eight agricultural regions, each with a Regional Agricultural Center (CAR) presided over by a director responsible to one of the vice-ministers. All Ministry operations in a region are under the control of the CAR director. In contrast, most of the other institutions have highly centralised operations, with the San José office controlling all policy decisions.

Beyond CANcitos, a local level semi-public institution existing in certain areas is the Cantonal Agricultural Committee. Composed of community members concerned with agricultural development, these committees can be funded, according to law, out of a specific tax on sugar cane production in each canton (county). The few cantons where these committees work vigorously have been, not surprisingly, those with significant sugar production. The committees in these areas work closely with the Ministry of Agriculture and other institutional staffs to promote agriculture in their areas. Activities include experimental farms, nurseries, demonstration projects, agricultural scholarships, and fish ponds.

INTERAGENCY COORDINATION IN THE URBAN SECTOR

Several interagency coordination efforts have been initiated in San José. In one large lower-class neighbourhood, all the principal public and private service agencies have been grouped together in the same physical facility and operate under an interagency committee structure to coordinate services. The PROVIS system, described in more detail below, also represents such a coordinated effort in low-cost housing. Additionally, the Costa Rican Community Development Agency (DINADECO) significantly increased its efforts in urban areas to strengthen both community based organisations and to coordinate public and private services focused on *tugurios*.[8]

Several points should be considered in trying to determine the type of structure which could serve the urban sector in a way similar to the CANcito system in rural areas.

1 Communities and cantons located in the San José Metropolitan Area are part of a large conurbation in which the physical, political, and institutional boundaries of municipal government have in effect ceased to be valid. Unlike their rural counterparts, urban municipalities are not the most important source of public services and their individual identities have been obscured in a large mass of urban structures which cross the limits of cantons, often making it difficult to say where one canton ends and the other begins, or which municipality should serve which barrio. Furthermore, urban municipalities are physically located in an area where they compete with larger public sector entities and where the population is accustomed to dealing with higher level sources of power. In other words, the concept of using the municipal unit as a focal point in developing a service structure to the urban poor does not appear to be fully acceptable.

2 Public sector agencies in the San José Metropolitan Area serve a wide variety of clients. Each socio-economic level faces problems peculiar to its immediate microcosm, in addition to those affecting the entire urban environment. Thus a standardised vertically integrated delivery system of services would not reflect the needs of the varied groups located at each income level.

3 The Costa Rican urban poor are close to the news media and are well informed about politics and the country's current situation. Literary and formal educational attainment are high. The effect on cooperation in community efforts cannot readily be foreseen.

4 Urban planning, defined in a broad sense beyond housing and infrastructure, is a new phenomenon in Costa Rica. Planners have to deal with a wide range of problems and complaints – city beautification, pollution, quality of life, alcoholism, crime, unemployment. These illustrate the complexity of dealing with the urban environment and the potential conflicts in trying to develop even a local consensus on priority needs.

5 One other aspect to be taken into account when trying to define an integral system of services for the urban poor is the way in which both the public entities and the beneficiaries perceive

each other's roles and responsibilities. One example is the Family Allowances Programme (Asignaciones Familiares) which relies heavily on community cooperation and volunteer work, and which has elicited local participation and a sense of pride and responsibility on the part of beneficiaries and volunteer workers. This may be due in large part to the promotion and motivation efforts of the Community Development Agency, DINADECO. The Ministry of the Presidency has tried to coordinate efforts addressed to alleviate urban poverty but appears to be dealing with the problem in a piecemeal basis, rather than as part of a larger, more comprehensive strategy which can coordinate substantial public investment and foreign capital inputs.

FINANCING SERVICES IN *TUGURIOS*

Ultimately, financing services in *tugurios* involves the specific identification of urban anti-poverty strategies, the types of institutions to carry them out, and the degree of self-finance sought. Clearly these are questions that deserve more attention than we can give them here.

One of the most complex questions deals with the incidence of taxation and subsidy schemes associated with anti-poverty programmes. The alternative burdens and benefits should be analysed with an eye both to their direct effects (especially the incidence of taxes on different income groups) and the indirect effects. Social charges against wages, ostensibly to benefit workers, give some incentive towards substitution of capital for the now more expensive labour.

Early attention should also be given to identifying 'outreach' institutions which presently are working well with poor communities, but which may lack official recognition by official aid agencies and technical assistance bureaus, and which may not be adept in selling themselves as recipients of public funds. We have already called attention to the problem of coordinating the role of the private sector in fighting urban poverty with the activities of the public sector. So too within the public sector itself, planners tend sometimes to overlook some very imaginative, cost-effective, and adaptable poverty interventions undertaken by small private and voluntary agencies or by community based groups.

SELF-FINANCING POVERTY PROGRAMMES: PROS AND CONS

Self-financed poverty programmes, based on pay-as-you-go principles, have obvious appeal in a world of scarce resources. They focus attention on the need for economy in designing programmes. Too many anti-poverty experiments have been very expensive and could have reached the total target population only by spending the entire national budget. Self-financed programmes encourage self-reliance. They thus mobilise untapped sources of local capital, local initiative, and local pride. They help avoid backlash from other income groups who may resent subsidising the poor. Finally, they emphasise productive activity, as opposed to mere transfer payments unassociated with output.

Whatever their appeal, however, self-finance has its own drawbacks. One of the most serious poses basic ethical questions of social justice. The poor are expected to pay their own way at the same time as a variety of government programmes directly and indirectly subsidise activities of middle- and upper-income groups.

The realism of self-finance has also been questioned. The scheme may work for people who have the motivation, education, health, family situation, location, and other circumstances that permit them to be productive when given the chance. Substantial numbers of the poor, however, do not fit this description, especially among the lowest incomes. For them, subsidised programmes are necessary supplements to self-financed schemes.

Even self-financed schemes usually require initial credit. If repayment falls behind, debt service can become an intolerable burden for the agency involved. But big deficits or outright bankruptcies of poverty-fighting agencies not only damage themselves, but may also jeopardise otherwise sound programmes by giving ammunition for criticism that would not arise in traditional subsidised programmes.

In Costa Rica, self-finance possibilities for urban infrastructure have been studied. They have not been applied to *tugurio* areas, although enabling legislation exists to allow them under contractual arrangements through the National Municipal Development Agency (IFAM). According to one study, the absence of complete ability to pay in *tugurios* could be compensated by extended payment terms or by other elements of (indirect) government subsidy.[9]

REGULATING THE CONSTRUCTION INDUSTRY

As a key element in alleviating (or reinforcing) Costa Rican urban poverty, residential construction deserves close attention. The problems associated with an historical build up of uncoordinated and sometime competing regulatory agencies are nowhere better illustrated. At this writing a single and unified construction code and earthquake safety code has not been adopted. Design and construction continue to be ruled by a body of unrelated standards, established on an *ad hoc* basis by different government institutions and municipalities. The necessary approval procedure is shown in Figure 8.1.[10]

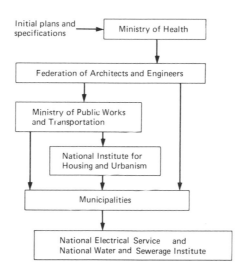

FIG. 8.1.   Flow chart of the necessary steps in obtaining construction permits

As shown, there are differing pathways to approval, depending upon the type of construction. All plans must be sent to both the Ministry of Health and the Federation of Architects and Engineers for approval. From there, they go directly to the Municipality, unless they are for buildings facing a National Highway which must be approved by the Ministry of Public Works and Transportation, or for a development project, which must be approved by the National Institute for Housing. It is the municipalities that are ultimately responsible for issuing construction permits and collecting taxes. They may set requirements on design and construction and hold up projects when considered appropriate. Approval is also needed from both the National Electrical Service and the National Water and Sewerage Institute, although this may be obtained after construction has begun.

Many persons both in the private and public sector consider that the frequent opposition by municipalities to the use of minimum construction standards adopted by the National Institute for Housing (INVU), for what it calls 'economical houses', is the greatest obstacle to more effective work in the field of low cost housing. The municipalities frequently allege that low cost housing turns into instant slums. They do not see that the lack of sufficient low-cost units leads to squatter settlements with no standards and no control. It is necessary that both the municipalities and other organisms understand that the standards for low-cost housing must be adjusted to the economic resources of the country and to the ability of the poor groups to pay. It is further necessary to expedite the project approval process for the construction of housing, particularly for the poor.

FINANCING HOUSING FOR THE URBAN POOR

Housing finance is similarly fragmented. Again, students of organisational history can detail the creation and evolution of institutions which, in time, come to have both overlaps and gaps. In 1977, we found no fewer than eight institutions or systems of institutions associated with providing housing for the urban poor, some only tangentially, others wholly. Costa Rica is hardly unique in this respect. The proliferation and partial duplication of these institutions might be considered beneficial if healthy inter-institutional competition were the outcome. So far as we could determine, however, none of the sources for housing finance thought competition desirable. Each would have been happy to be the monopolist, whether state-sponsored or private, in its own segment of the market.

National banking system

Commercial banking in Costa Rica is state-owned, the result of the nationalisation of four formerly private country-wide banking chains. The commercial banks get loanable funds for housing from deposits, repayments of previous loans, and in a single case from the Central American Bank for Economic Integration. Conventional mortgage terms are used. For Costa Rica, this means an interest rate of 9 or 10 per cent on a loan not exceeding 60 to 75 per cent of the appraised value of the dwelling, to a maximum of ₡140,000, and a ten-year repayment period. While the precise income distribution of the borrowers is unknown, the size of the average loan (in 1976) of more than ₡100,000 and the unsubsidised repayment terms suggest that only upper-income recipients could afford repayment.

Savings and loan system

The state-sponsored system was created in 1969 to encourage thrift and to increase the flow of funds into residential construction for families of low and middle income. The system has been financed largely by loans from the Central American Bank for Economic Integration, rather than through savings deposits. The system has also sold mortgage participation to private institutions and individuals. Loans are made only to persons with a savings account. Interest rates are 11 or 13.75 per cent for less and more expensive houses, respectively. Repayment periods can last for twenty-five years and a loan on as much as 90 per cent of a house's appraised value can be obtained. The system seems to have had some success in reaching its target population. While the highest authorisable loan is ₡85,400 ($10,000), 78 per cent of the loans have been less than ₡60,000 and 42 per cent less than ₡42,000.

Social Assistance Institute (IMAS)

This institute is a public autonomous institution of the type mentioned previously in this chapter. It was created in 1971 to help resolve the socio-economic problems of the poor. Its operating mandate extends well beyond housing. Its sources of funds are various; they include a payroll tax, profits from the operation of free port stores, and a motel tax, as well as a direct subsidy from the central government. The allocation of houses has been based on the demonstrated needs of the recipients, rather than on their ability to repay a standard loan. No down payment is required, and other loan terms have been flexible, depending on the incomes of the residents. In the majority of cases, borrowers have not repaid amounts sufficient to cover the costs of lending. The Institute, in an interesting and perhaps paternalistic gesture, retains titles to the homes it builds.

National Institute of Housing and Urbanism (INVU)

This Institute has been the largest organisation directly involved in Costa Rican housing. Completely state-owned, it has constructed housing projects for sale and for rent, has made loans to finance new construction and the purchase of already constructed homes, and has engaged in urban land development for the sale of dwelling lots. The Institute receives financial support from the sale of its own bonds, from interest and amortisation on loans it has made, from the sale of homes and lots, and to a lesser extent from the Central American Bank for Economic Integration. Some subsidised loans are made to low-income purchasers, but title is retained by the Institute for a period of five years. While low-cost housing has comprised about one-third of the Institute's activities, few are within the reach of persons below the twentieth percentile in the income distribution, and 60 per cent are held by those above the 40th percentile.

Integrated Programme of Social Interest Housing (PROVIS)

The Programme is one result of an inter-institutional agreement, in which the National Institute for Housing (INVU), the Institute for Social Assistance (IMAS), and the Agency for Community Development (DINADECO) participated. It has sought to combine funds from INVU and IMAS in dealing with the housing problem for low-income families. The Programme has no independent investment in housing. Its target group has been defined as families with incomes less than ₡1,400 ($164) per month. Along with some other institutions working with the poor, it has presented housing not as an end in itself, but rather as a means to increase the productive capacity of the poor. It has worked not with isolated families, but only with previously organised community groups. Self-help housing programmes have formed the centre of a larger programme whose interests lie in convincing groups of their collective capability to solve their own problems.

Social Security Fund (CCSS)

The Costa Rican social security system has purchased mortgages directly and has made investments, as well, in the bonds of the National Institute for Housing (INVU). Conventional mortgage terms are the rule, and loans have gone predominantly to families of medium and higher incomes.

National Insurance Institute (INS)

Like the social security system, the state-owned insurance institute seeks portfolio investments. About 55 per cent of its total capital has been invested in mortgage loans. Only its policy holders are eligible to receive loans, which tips the bulk of them away from low-cost houses and low-income families.

The People's Communal Development Bank

The Bank was established in 1969 as a credit source for low-income workers. About half its loans have been for housing. Its sources of funds have included a payroll tax and voluntary savings deposits. As with the savings and loan system, only depositors are eligible for loans. Repayment periods of up to twenty years soften the exigencies of interest rates that may run to 12 per cent. Lower and middle income families are the chief beneficiaries of the bank's loans, as indicated by the average size of loan of ₡42,000 in 1976.

HOUSING FINANCE AND URBAN DEVELOPMENT POLICY

State activity in housing has continuously increased during the twentieth century. Nevertheless, no central body has ever coordinated the work of these financial (or other) agencies. The absence of consistent and rational guidance has led, in turn, to a number of anomalies.

Some duplication of functions exists. In the absence of well-defined and executed priorities, middle- and upper-income groups are favoured, even by many state-sponsored or state-owned financial organisations. The agencies that deal most directly with the poor also bear the reputation of having the least technical ability.

Problems of measurement hinder systematic assays of the housing problem, even when it is viewed as a relatively self-contained phenomenon. The size of the housing deficit, for example, is uncomfortably sensitive to definitions of the adequacy of a dwelling's physical characteristics. Statistics on ability-to-pay of the various income strata depend on accurate collection of data on the income distribution.

The presence of more than a single agency dealing with housing for the poor has also led to divergence among their policies. While the National Institute for Housing (INVU) makes some loans at 13 per cent interest, other agencies such as the National Insurance Institute lends to higher income individuals at considerably lower interest rates. These differentials may reflect the costs of loanable funds (INVU's come partly from abroad, while the Insurance Institute's are domestic) and the element of risk in lending to persons of low incomes; nevertheless, there have been no explicit policy pronouncements wrestling with the fact that the poor pay higher rates.

The situation presented in this section and the previous one leads us to suggest that a systematic and overall view of urban housing for the poor would allow a more effective use of scarce resources. We do not advocate more (or less) state-sponsored activity, nor are we disdainful of the strides already made on behalf of low-cost housing. We note simply that the variety of institutions – operating in a world of growing complexity, and evolving in unforeseen ways – make an overall survey attractive. Such a survey would likely lead to a national housing plan.

Such a plan need not lead automatically to greater income redistribution, taking the form of greater benefits for the urban poor. The present situation of overlaps and anomalies may permit, through the confusion created for public opinion, more redistribution than would be allowed by an informed public. This is a risk, however, that we would be willing to assume under the institutional circumstances outlined in such detail above.

CONCLUSIONS

A national housing plan is only a single element in a more comprehensive urban and regional development plan of the sort alluded to above. It requires resolution of the same sorts of problems facing all planners: questions of optimal levels of centralisation, of the proper role for the state, of the creation of effective incentives, and of the inclusion in public life of an appropriately wide variety of opinions and interests. As a focus for inquiry, concern with urban poverty has more frequently centred on the housing problem. This chapter has shown the wider field surrounding the mere provision of physical shelter.

9 Conclusions

Urban poverty and its assessment vary according to time and setting. Generalisation is no easier in this field than in other avenues of social scientific inquiry. Our empirical studies in Costa Rica, however, in some cases suggest and in others reinforce a series of general conclusions widely applicable in Third World countries and possibly beyond.

In this book, we have tried to show that in poverty analysis an emphasis on geographical units (cities, regions, neighbourhoods) is inappropriate. Instead a focus on poor people rather than on poor places is more likely to accomplish the goals of the poor and of agencies seeking to improve their lot.

For the problems of urban poverty, a multiplicity of analytical approaches exists. They are not mutually exclusive. Therefore, rather than selecting the single most useful one, we suggest that they should be jointly considered and applied, since they represent varied and useful insights into poverty, both as a condition and as a process.

Normative approaches to urban poverty usually rely on project evaluation techniques. However, especially for 'soft' and unbankable projects (those for which conventional bank loans are not readily forthcoming), these techniques are still at an early stage in their methodological development. Thus, as an alternative, we are convinced that review and imitation of past successes, no matter what their original prospects appeared to be, will be more effective than the selection of projects based on the imperfect social benefit–cost techniques now available. By extension, this implies that inductive approaches to development analysis would usefully supplement, but not displace, the more common deductive ones.

Costa Rican data presented in Chapter 3 lead us to conclude that the negative characteristics of urban migrants have been vastly exaggerated. The exaggeration has led, in turn, to misplaced concern over the impact of the migration process. We found that migrants to San José share many of the characteristics of the urban population they joined. Evidence was also presented to show that migrants did not reside disproportionately in urban slums. These findings are consistent with those of other Latin American countries, lending them greater validity and generality.

Urbanisation in developing countries is most easily characterised as a rapid increase in numbers living in cities. In small countries, the capital city is the most prominent target. Rapid urbanisation does indeed involve negative externalities. Congestion and pollution are the most common examples. But our findings should be interpreted properly: the negative externalities associated with rapid urban growth (only part of which, incidentally, is the result of urban migration) are not caused by the characteristics of migrants. The importance of this conclusion can hardly be over-emphasised, since policy decisions are so frequently based on what we have shown to be incorrect premises.

It may be instructive to consider hypothetically the nature of urban poverty in the absence of urban migration. Cities would still grow at rapid rates, owing to the natural increase in population by their residents, although the rates would, as a rule of thumb, be about half those currently observed. The city's poor would still be there and would live in physically substandard conditions in the city's centre. And to the extent that potential migrants, bottled up in rural areas and unable to move to cities, were themselves poor, their remaining in the countryside would mean simply that poverty's location was different and not that its extent was any less.

In Chapter 4 we looked at employment. While the original locus of interest lay in physically deteriorated areas, *tugurios*, we concluded that the unemployed were not notably concentrated in these areas. This finding, while perhaps counterintuitive, is consistent with the notion of the operation of labour markets at the level of the city as a whole, rather than a series of spatially separated labour markets, some in poor neighbourhoods and others elsewhere. In fact, the direct and indirect evidence cited in the chapter supports the conclusion that labour markets in the metropolitan area operated with reasonable articulation. The policy implication of this finding has already been noted, and in fact it is central to this study: it is more effective in analysing and dealing with poverty to focus on poor people and the reasons behind their low incomes than to adopt a spatial orientation that focuses on the improvement of run-down neighbourhoods.

The census and survey data especially commissioned for this study also led to conclusions about the effects of employment and training on overcoming poverty. Employment-oriented solutions (and associated training) will provide some poor people with opportunities to increase their incomes at the same time as their output rises. But the poorest will still be excluded from improvement, and will need transfer payments if their lot is to be improved. Bureaucrats and bankers alike tend to avoid these conclusions, since the recommendations that follow smack of charity rather than self-financed self-help, and thus collide with the understandable biases of most of those actively involved in working with poor people. Nevertheless, for a substantial proportion of the poor (those, say, in the lowest 10 or even 20 per cent of income receivers), job creation programmes benefiting the majority (those able and willing to work for pay) will not be effective. Employment programmes, whatever their benefits, will widen existing inequalities in the income distribution, and will distract attention from the plight of those at the bottom.

Assessment of poverty mixes positive and normative elements, the descriptive with the prescriptive, as Chapters 5, 6, and 7 made clear. Prescriptions are usually implicitly included in descriptions, since our descriptive models have usually been formulated in an environment in which improvements in human welfare are seen as central. The varieties of assessment methods reflect the differences in training and emphasis of the analysts involved. Thus economists focus on scarcity and on financial aspects, urban anthropologists on social adaptation mechanisms of closely observed low-income city dwellers, political scientists on ways in which political opinions are filtered through institutional hierarchies and made operational, and so on. In addition, the variety of currently existing assessment methods reflects an historic accumulation. Our understanding of processes that create and maintain poverty has itself evolved as experience grows and the empirical testing of scientific theories proceeds.

We have presented six approaches to the assessment of poverty as complements rather than substitutes for one another. The question, 'What is the best single measure of poverty?' seems to pander to the simplistic and reductionist urges that we all possess and that we all should resist. To be sure, each of the six approaches can be misused, and has been on occasion in the past. That is to say, not one of them is immune to an ignorant or malevolent misinterpretation. At the same time, we are convinced that each one embodies a useful point of view.

Poor countries and the regions within them have been conventionally identified with low incomes per capita. As a summary measure, that statistic has been widely collected and disseminated. Its lack of concern either with sources of income or with its distribution may obscure its usefulness as a first step in locating the poor. The market basket approach to drawing poverty lines goes beyond the per capita income measurements. The cost of a minimal market basket, sometimes described as the minimum income associated with so-called basic needs, can be calculated, and the numbers of people earning or receiving less than this amount can also be counted.

Subjective elements are always present in the establishment of the appropriate contents of the market basket. Prices of these elements will vary from place to place. The measurement problems, in short, are greater than those associated with per capita income, and the judgemental nature of determining 'needs' upsets scientists who insist on strict experimental replicability. Nevertheless, as long as the needs are clearly stated, observers are free to modify them, and therefore to change the proportions of the population classified as falling under one or another of the established poverty lines.

A more subtle and sophisticated assessment comes in the form of income distribution measures. These measurements, whether taking the form of a summary statistics such as a Gini coefficient or even more simply stated as the proportion of income received by the bottom (or top) x per cent of income earners, focus on relative income rather than on the absolute size of the amount received or on its purchasing power. As a result, these measurements are sometimes dismissed on grounds that are superficially logical but that lack insight into the human condition. If the bottom 20 or 40 per cent of the income receivers are defined as 'poor', then it is arithmetically correct that the poor will always be with us. But given the increasing tendency to compare one's income with others, either to close neighbours or (thanks to decreased costs of information transmission) to people who live half a world away, it matters very much whether the bottom 40 per cent receive 30 per cent of the nation's income or 10 per cent. In formal terms, we should recognise the tendency of individuals to include relative incomes in their welfare or utility functions. The psychological importance of 'relative deprivation' has not yet been widely recognised by economic textbooks that generally postulate an individual's welfare as dependent on his own consumption and leisure, but not on the attributes of other persons. Once again, we do not advocate the exclusive use of either summary or disaggregated income distributional measures to assess poverty. At the same time, we think them worthy of careful consideration, complementing the other assessment methods.

Turning attention away from measures that consider money incomes and money costs, a series of social indicators permit poverty assessment at still another level. While economists have been clever in assigning money values to literacy and health, direct observations of these and other social indicators cuts through the shortcomings of economic imputation. Each of the indicators we ultimately choose is implicitly connected with our notions of poverty. We think of 'poor' people as those who can't read, or who have little chance of celebrating their fortieth birthday, or who have no access to radio and television, or who cannot readily travel to nearby towns, or who live in substandard housing.

Remedies for these deficiencies are implied by the measurements themselves. Where social indicators show poverty, we usually try to improve those aspects of life that are measured. Such an approach puts great pressure on the initial selection and definition of the variables to be measured. If the measured variables themselves are the only targets for amelioration, then our concern that they represent priority areas becomes large indeed.

A later development in poverty assessment has recognised the benefits involved in access to capital, whether economic or social. Rural credit programmes, for example, do not deal directly with poverty if the only credit-worthy borrowers are large landowners. Extending access to credit to the poor may be costly, but poverty is indicated by a current lack of access. Other areas of access to capital include human capital in the form of education and health facilities. Access to social institutions is also a poverty indicator. Some of poverty's most bitter aspects lie in the absence of opportunity for improvement that frustrates impulses toward advancement. Extending opportunity is implicit in the extension of access to capital. It is appropriate to note in this concluding chapter that the question of access to capital (or to opportunity) is one of the less studied and understood areas of intellectual inquiry and of administrative practice. While the notion as we have stated it above seems quite clear, its detailed specification and qualified application to action programmes still lies in the future. Finally, we urged that poverty be assessed in an historical perspective. The desirability of doing so seems clear. Rich countries themselves have undergone development since the Second World War. Their notions of the nature of desirable development, both past and future, have evolved. For example, factory chimneys belching smoke, once a sign of great wealth, are now shunned in rich countries. Women working outside the home for pay, formerly identified with great economic hardship (depression) or with pressing national needs (war), now have changed their image. Toward which aspects of development ought poor countries and poor people to be striving? If in 1955 they started along a path of development that imitated the rich countries of that time, they would have found a quarter-century later that their development was oriented toward a now obsolete set of goals. The only offset to these difficulties is an historical perspective that keeps clearly in mind changes in goals, changes in constraints, and changes in opportunities that confront the world's poor, and those who feel themselves drawn to pay attention to them.

Even when the analysis of poverty has been flawless, the translation of analysis into policy and action must pass through the sieve of public administration. Some of the issues were reviewed in Chapter 8. Urban and regional planning is in its infancy in low-income countries, although national plans based on national economic aggregates have been reasonably well refined. The administrative difficulties include problems of incorporating grass-roots opinion, of taking initiative, and of coordinating numerous and powerful semi-autonomous agencies. The agencies and ministries of the executive branch are supposed, of course, to be working in common towards well established goals, but individual ambition and the demands of politics (both within the government and outside it) often obstruct the interagency relations whose complications are neglected in textbook treatments.

Implementation of policy decisions at a decentralised level can only be effective when technical knowledge and financial resources are combined with the delegation of responsibility to make decisions. Each of these three requirements (knowledge, resources, responsibility) has been ignored at one time or another in the past, to the detriment of the eventual outcome. Each is a necessary condition for success.

Even such mundane matters as political boundaries can cause problems. As cities grow and extend their boundaries, the political subdivisions of a country, reflecting historical decisions and compromises rather than current realities, may be dysfunctional as units around which to base developmental agencies. Here financial resources are likely to be decisive. An agency that spans more than a single political boundary, combining municipalities and suburban areas, can work if it is well financed by the central government, and will flounder if it depends on the voluntary contributions and moral support of the participating local governments.

Our findings show as well that socially beneficent moves are obstructed by the nature of the process through which they must pass. The proliferation and duplication of agencies associated, for example, with the issuance of construction permits and with financing housing for the poor remind us that political territoriality (protecting one's 'turf') has the same priority in anti-poverty institutions that it does in less idealistic organisations.

ADDITIONAL PERSPECTIVES ON POVERTY

This book has dealt with urban poverty and economic development from a broad perspective, considering several measures of poverty and several policy areas for assisting the poor. Nevertheless, no single study can be wholly adequate, especially in applying analytical findings to action in particular communities. In closing this study, let us briefly remark on its limitations, and on ways to supplement it by other considerations necessary for policy formation.

As professional analysts, we try to stand back and view our subject impartially, describing poverty in objective terms, scrutinising its causes, and generalising from particulars. Yet poverty can be characterised as involuntary deprivation, and has both material and psychic elements. It is therefore more than simply an objective phenomenon to be readily inspected and described. It concerns human lives, expectations, and struggles that cannot be understood by statistical indicators alone.

In this study, we have relied a great deal on a series of economic definitions of poverty. At the same time, we realise that economic categories maintain poverty as an abstraction, as well as keeping the lives of poor people at a distance. Poverty has experiential qualities that do not issue clear signals when one crosses a predetermined 'poverty line'. Poverty lines refer to quantities of possessions, services, and consumables that provide a subsistence living standard. But if we consider poverty as involuntary deprivation, then it also incorporates a state of mind and a condition of being that transcend material conditions. Taken alone, the data reveal very little about why some people are poor and not others, or why some can and do take advantage of the limited opportunities available and others cannot.

Our earlier chapters with their quantitative analysis help to describe poor people in the aggregate. Careful statistical analysis is especially important in Costa Rica. As we have shown, that country's poor blend easily into the rest of society, in terms of their spatial distribution, racial homogeneity, access to services and opportunities to enter the steadily growing modern sector. Only by analysing census data or specially designed surveys, as we did, does exclusion of the poorest groups from the overall picture of successful progress become clear. The lowest 20 per cent are not rising with the mainstream of development. The gap is widening rather than closing. Such findings are increasingly common in the study of the poorest countries. However, they seem more surprising in a country like Costa Rica which has undertaken remarkably progressive social policies on behalf of its poor.

Objective analysis helps every observer to see this disturbing situation. It seldom, perhaps never, explains its causes clearly enough to overcome them. It is important to show the existence of persistent poverty as a distinct but integral part of development that would otherwise be labelled 'successful'. Such a demonstration stimulates planners to look behind conventional measures of success embodied in national averages or regional indicators of modernisation.

While we have studied the spatial distribution and social incidence of poverty, it is also important to weigh its significance as a qualitative experience. In the end, development strategies should be chosen (but, alas, seldom are) by comparing relative priorities among competing social and economic objectives. Merely recognising poverty's existence cannot influence policies unless decision makers are willing to contrast the net benefits of poverty programmes with the more familiar advantages of modern sector investments. But in this context, many of the costs of poverty do not lend themselves to easy measurement. They are nevertheless worth considering carefully: the costs levied on human dignity both among the poor and those who live alongside them; the costs reflected in a nation's self-image; the costs experienced by individuals who have not chosen to be hungry, cold, sick, unemployed, or unable to care for their families.

These terms suggest that poverty can be understood as an experience. Biographies may reveal more than statistical patterns. Poverty in this sense may not submit to logic, reason, or ready explanation. It incorporates and expresses the illogic, hopelessness, and resentment poor people feel about their present situation and most importantly, about their chances for improvement. It cannot be derived from analysing aggregates, but requires seeing individual reactions to the adversity of circumstances. Some people actively and successfully overcome their initial disadvantages; others passively cope or tragically succumb. Seen in this way, poverty cannot be understood merely by documenting the present or the past. Instead, we must assess the character of poor people's most constructive expectations and tap these as guides to the design of real opportunities.

Perhaps an effective poverty strategy does not exist. As we have taken pains to point out, poverty is not a single problem and it therefore cannot have a single cure. Any economic indicator of poverty is only a symptom of myriad circumstances affecting people's well-being. Groups with the same symptoms, as measured by these economic indicators, may nevertheless have very different propensities for improvement. In particular, some groups are poised to use outside assistance effectively, since their expectations, skills and organisation are well adapted to capitalising on newly supplied information, financial resources, and productive assets. Other groups are simply not mobilised for change. Few poverty programmes distinguish between groups that need help and can use it, groups that need it but cannot absorb it, and groups that usually get help, owing to their organisation and connections, but who for the same reason need it least.

Another problem in defining an overall poverty strategy concerns the fallacy of aggregates. Areal statistics give the impression of poor people moving as a single mass in slow increments, generally towards improvement, though often slipping back in periods of adversity. A closer (more disaggregated) look at individual life trajectories of the poor, however, yields a quite different impression. In an unregimented system with high geographic and social mobility for some individuals, poor people often rise up suddenly, making personal breakthroughs with the help of networks of friends and agencies, and at the same time detaching themselves from the fate of their peers. While on average, progress comes in slow, painful gradients, for any individual it is marked by breakouts and sudden changes in attitudes, expectations, and real opportunities. Poverty strategies influenced only by aggregate statistics fail to capitalise on the rhythms of individual life cycles in a developmental setting, which can be marked by unforeseen capacities for individual and cooperative effort. Poverty programmes, however, are usually designed to minimise risk. They therefore impose a model of 'correct' action that restrains those ready to move ahead at the same time that it seems too ambitious for those who are not.

We conclude that a theory of poverty must really be a theory of plural poverties. Policy should be guided by a theory of contingent actions suited to the variations in poverty. Some aspects of poverty call for basic structural changes aimed at lowering barriers to opportunity. Poverty everywhere has a discernible relation to age, sex, race or ethnic background, and geographic location. Poverty's causes may derive from social prejudice or tradition, unequal access to power, psychological dependence, concentrationist tendencies of economic organisation, segmentation of labour markets, legal regulations, or market mechanisms that favour established groups. These factors remain untouched by most poverty strategies, yet they play an important part in weakening the outcomes of such efforts.

Other causes and cures of poverty are more practical and immediate, however, and have clearer implications for local, self-initiated action. To be sure, poverty programmes need to be constructed in a context of fundamental changes and long-term policies. Yet elaborate plans risk removing people's destinies from their control and imposing instead the opinions of outside experts with their supposedly greater grasp of possible solutions.

On close observation, poor people often reveal themselves to be resourceful, tenacious, and rational in managing their affairs using quite limited means. Strategies can be devised to take greater advantage of these qualities. Elements of such a strategy can be found in the recent literature of basic needs and self-help approaches to development. Tactically these approaches suggest greater emphasis on *ad hoc* public grants responsive to locally initiated development projects, as opposed to categorical programmes governed by the priorities of outside agencies.

The theory and practice of cooperative organisation and community development go in and out of fashion, but their basic message – that people do best who can help themselves – is repeatedly rediscovered. Technical assistance agencies are uncomfortable with this lesson, because of their customary isolation from the actual sites where such lessons are painfully learned and relearned. Perhaps too, donor agencies, as givers rather than receivers, naturally presume that their possession of superior resources gives them superior wisdom too about how resources ought to be used in any given community. That presumption is, of course, a grave fallacy.

One lesson that must be continually reabsorbed is the need for two-way learning about poverty between poor communities and assistance agencies. In principle, each could show the other neglected opportunities and areas for advance. The most important missing ingredient in policy design seems to be the incorporations of how poor people perceive their own needs and their own possible solutions.

The time may have come for treatises on poverty by the poor themselves, who can speak equally of problems and successes, mistakes and lessons learned, patience for long-term solutions and justifiable impatience with the pace and direction of present assistance programmes. In these respects, we still have much to learn from the people of Costa Rica and from others who have worked to give the poor a voice in directing their own efforts to self-improvement.

Notes

CHAPTER 1

1. International Labour Office, *Poverty and Landlessness in Rural Asia* (Geneva: ILO, 1977).
2. International Labour Office, *A Basic-Needs Strategy for Africa* (Geneva: ILO, 1977).
3. There are a variety of short-cut techniques available, though most are not widely known, such as IMPASSE (IMPact ASSEssment gaming), dialectical scanning, the Delbecq group process technique, cross-impact modelling, and Delphi. Most of these feature a high degree of participation in assessing multiple outcomes from policy proposals. See Dean Runyan, 'Tools for Community-Managed Impact Assessment', *Journal of the American Institute of Planning*, vol. 43, no. 2 (April 1977) pp. 125–35.
4. Population Reference Bureau, '1977 World Population Fact Sheet' (Washington, DC: Population Reference Bureau, 1977).
5. Robert W. Fox and Jerrold W. Huguet, *Population and Urban Trends in Central America and Panama* (Washington, D.C.: Inter-American Development Bank, 1977) pp. 58–83.
6. The greater Metropolitan Area is made up on the Central Canton of the province of San José and ten surrounding cantons in its zone of immediate influence. Excepted are certain sub-districts which, for reasons of topography or excessive distance, do not offer possibilities for integration with this central nucleus.
7. Manuel J. Carvajal and David T. Geithman, 'An Economic Analysis of Migration in Costa Rica', *Economic Development and Cultural Change*, vol. 23, no. 1 (October 1974) pp. 105–22.

CHAPTER 2

1. F. Zumbado and L. B. Neuhauser have made a useful study of eight agricultural area cantons, four of them characterised by expulsion, the other four by attraction. It would take further analysis, however, to extrapolate their findings to the country as a whole. See their chapter, 'Evolución de la Distribución de la Población en Costa Rica', in Manuel J. Carvajal (ed.), *Políticas de Crecimiento Urbano* (San José: Dirección de Estadísticas y Censos, 1977) pp. 68–110.
2. Manuel J. Carvajal and David T. Geithman, 'An Economic Analysis of Migration in Costa Rica', *Economic Development and Cultural Change*, vol. 23, no. 1 (October 1974) pp. 105–22.

3. Robert W. Fox and Jerrold W. Huguet, *Demographic Trends and Urbanization in Costa Rica* (Washington, D.C.: Inter-American Development Bank, 1975).
4. F. Zumbado and L. B. Neuhauser, 'Evolución de la Distribución de la Población en Costa', op. cit.
5. Costa Rica, Oficina de Planificación, *Estrategia de Desarrollo Regional* (San José, 1975) p. 50.
6. See, for example, United Nations Centre for Regional Development, *Growth Pole Strategy and Regional Planning in Asia*, Proceedings of a seminar, Nagoya, Japan: UNCRD, 1975.
7. Zumbado and Neuhauser, op. cit., p. 97.
8. A small portion of this employment is probably located outside the Metropolitan Area, in other parts of San José Province, but this breakdown of data is not available. The figure for the Agglomeration as a whole is probably in the range of 80 to 90 per cent. Becaux (in the work cited in Table 2.6, para. 1.23) arrived at the figure of 89 per cent by adding the data for San José Province to industrial employment figures for the other major cities in the Agglomeration, namely Alajuela, Cartago, and Heredia. Each of these three cities is the capital of a province which fans out to the country's borders from the administrative headquarters clustered in the urban nucleus. For this reason, it is extremely misleading to use provincial level data to describe the spatial distribution of activities in Costa Rica, since four of the seven provinces have their economic and political centres of gravity within the Urban Agglomeration. Only the remaining three provinces – Puntarenas, Limón and Guanacaste – have their capitals outside the Agglomeration.
9. Zumbado and Neuhauser, op. cit., p. 103.
10. Ibid., p. 105.

CHAPTER 3

1. Conferencia dictada en el Seminario sobre Proceso de Metropolización en Costa Rica y América Latina. Escuela de Historia y Geografía, Universidad de Costa Rica, 16 de agosto al 17 de setiembre de 1976.
2. An appendix to chap. 4 gives some details about the survey.
3. The index of schooling is defined as the number of completed years of schooling divided by 11, the number of years in the Costa Rican primary and secondary educational system.
4. See Bruce Herrick, 'Urbanization and Urban Migration in Latin America: An Economist's View', in Francine F. Rabinowitz and Felicity M. Trueblood (eds), *Latin American Urban Research*, vol. 1 (Beverly Hills, California: Sage Publications, 1971).
5. OFIPLAN, *Metas de Progreso* (Plan Nacional de Desarrollo 1978–82), Versión Preliminar (San José: Oficina de Planificación Nacional y Política Económica, 1977) pp. 116–17.
6. Carlos Raabe, Oficina de Planificación, private communication, 8 September 1977.

CHAPTER 4

1. These matters are discussed in general in the works of Chenery and Kuznets. See, for example, Hollis Chenery and Moises Syrquin, *Patterns of Development, 1950–1970* (New York: Oxford University Press, 1975), pp. 48–53; Simon Kuznets, *Six Lectures on Economic Growth* (New York: Free Press, 1959), pp. 43–67; and Kuznets, *Economic Growth of Nations* (Cambridge, Mass.: Harvard University Press, 1971) pp. 199–302.

2. These figures have been derived from Tables 4.A.1 and 4.A.2 using rounded figures for output. For the three years under observation, labour productivity was: 1963 = ₡13,700, 1973 = ₡19,581, 1976 = ₡18,616. Note that these figures are calculated in terms of colones of 1966.

3. The ILO's World Employment Programme has used this framework extensively. See, among others, Amartya Sen, *Employment, Technology, and Development* (New York: Oxford University Press, 1975) esp. ch. 1.

4. Of the adults who said they would like to work (only housewives or 17 per cent of all adults surveyed), 4 per cent wanted to work full-time and 13 per cent part-time.

5. Category of present or formerly employed workers:

Permanent employee	65%
Temporary employee	8%
Self-employed and other	8%
Sub-total	81% of sample

6. Another possibility is somewhat less comfortable. It suggests that the surveyors were less than diligent in carrying out that part of the survey which inquired about alternative sources of income. Regardless of the reason, the survey's findings ought to be seriously considered, precisely because of their unexpectedness.

7. Feeling of lack of training:

Yes	12%
No	36%
No response	2%
	50% of sample

which was the total proportion of workers, excluding self-employed.

CHAPTER 5

1. International Labour Office, *The Basic-Needs Approach to Development* (Geneva: ILO, 1977).

2. See, for example, Lester Thurow, 'Toward a Definition of Economic Justice', *The Public Interest*, vol. 31 (Spring 1973) pp. 67–9.

3. For a discussion of methods, and review of some methodological pitfalls, see D. G. Champernowne, 'A Comparison of Measures of Inequality of Income Distribution', *Economic Journal* (December 1974), and F. A. Cowell, *Measuring Inequality* (New York: John Wiley, 1977). Shail Jain presents results for eighty-one countries in his *Size Distribution of Income* (Washington, D.C.: World Bank, 1975).
4. Inter-American Foundation, *They Know How* (Washington, D.C.: US Government Printing Office, 1977).
5. Planning and Development Collaborative International (PADCO), 'Social and Economic Components in Support of Housing Guarantee Projects', mimeo (Washington, D.C.: 1976).
6. Arthur F. Raper, *Rural Development in Action* (Ithaca: Cornell University Press, 1970). Charles Hampden-Turner, *From Poverty to Dignity* (Garden City, New York: Anchor Books, 1975).

CHAPTER 6

1. PADCO, 'Social and Economic Components in Support of Housing Guarantee Projects', mimeo (Washington, D.C.: 1976).
2. Irma Adelman and Cynthia Taft Morris, *Economic Growth and Social Equity in Developing Countries* (Stanford, California: Stanford University Press, 1973). Costa Rican data are from UN/ECLA, *Economic Survey of Latin America, 1969* (New York: United Nations, 1970) p. 366.
3. Shail Jain, *Size Distribution of Income: A Compilation of Data* (Washington, D.C.: World Bank, 1975).
4. cf. Hollis Chenery and Moises Syrquin, *Patterns of Development, 1950–1970* (New York: Oxford University Press, 1975).

CHAPTER 7

1. Inter-American Foundation, *They Know How* (Washington, D.C.: US Government Printing Office, 1977).
2. Charles Hampden-Turner, *From Poverty to Dignity* (Garden City, New York: Anchor Books, 1975).
3. Citations include William Mangin, 'Latin American Squatter Settlements: A Problem and a Solution', *Latin American Research Review*, vol. 2, no. 3 (Summer 1967) pp. 65–98. Oscar Lewis, 'Urbanization Without Breakdown: A Case Study', *The Scientific Monthly*, vol. 75 (1952) pp. 31–41. Kenneth Karst, Murray Schwartz and Audrey Schwartz, *The Evolution of Law in the Barrios of Caracas* (Los Angeles: Latin American Center, University of California, 1973).
4. Richard Ornstein, ed., *The Nature of Human Consciousness* (San Francisco: W. H. Freeman, 1973).
5. The data in Table 7.4 show responses to the specific question, 'In a case where the Government is not treating you justly, which mechanism do you think would produce fastest results?'

6. Mumford, *The City in History – Its Origins, Its Transformations, and Its Prospects* (New York: Harcourt, Brace and World, 1961); *The Pentagon of Power*, vol. II of *The Myth of the Machine* (New York: Harcourt Brace Jovanovich, 1970). Jacobs, *The Death and Life of Great American Cities* (New York: Random House, 1961). Howard, *Garden Cities of Tomorrow* (Cambridge, Mass.: MIT Press, 1965; first published 1898). We note parenthetically that the title 'Garden Cities' does not describe the book's contents well. The book was an attempt to compile historical precedents for economic, administrative, and spatial design of cities that would provide greater correspondence between those who pay for services and those who derive benefits from them.

7. See, for example, United Nations Centre for Regional Development, *Growth Pole Strategy and Regional Planning in Asia*, Proceedings of a seminar, Nagoya, Japan: UNCRD, 1975.

8. Dudley Seers, 'The Meaning of Development', *International Development Review*, vol. 9, no. 4 (Dec. 1969) pp. 2–6; reprinted, same journal, vol. 19, no. 2, 1977, pp. 2–7. John Friedmann and Clyde Weaver, *Territory and Function: The Evolution of Regional Planning* (London: Edward Arnold, 1979). Michael Lipton, *Why Poor People Stay Poor – Urban Bias in World Development* (London: Maurice Temple-Smith, 1977).

9. John Friedmann, 'Basic Needs, Agropolitan Development, and Planning from Below', *World Development*, vol. 7, no. 6 (June 1979). John Friedmann and Mike Douglass, 'Agropolitan Development: Towards a New Strategy for Regional Planning in Asia', in Fu-chen Lo and Kamal Saleh (eds), *Growth Pole Strategy and Regional Development Policy: Asian Experiences and Alternative Approaches* (Oxford: Pergamon Press, 1978).

CHAPTER 8

1. Translated from OFIPLAN, *Metas de Progreso* op. cit., pp. 116–17.

2. Miguel E. Morales, 'Región Central: Documentos de Avance', San José: División de Planificación Regional y Urbana, OFIPLAN, mimeo (National Planning Office, 1977).

3. Ibid., pp. 8ff.

4. Bernard Becaux, 'The Industrial Sector in Costa Rica', mimeo (San José, 1977).

5. A series of documents published by the National Planning Office in 1977 deal with these matters. See its 'Desarrollo Regional y Urbano' (March 1977), 'La Planificación Regional en Costa Rica' (1977), and 'Región Central: Elementos de Diagnóstico' (July 1977).

6. See also the remarks on ITCO's role and potential in Fernando Zumbado and Lydia B. Neuhauser, 'Evolución de la Distribución de la Población en Costa Rica', in Manuel J. Carvajal (ed.), *Politicas de Crecimiento Urbano* (San José, Dirección de Estadística y Censos, 1977) p. 108.

7. Charles Hampden-Turner, *From Poverty to Dignity* (Garden City, New York: Anchor Books, 1975).

8. Before 1967, various Costa Rican government institutions had small offices involved in community development, with resulting loss of resources and multiplicity of efforts. DINADECO was formed to remedy this situation by centralising community development in Costa Rica with the help of specialised personnel, community level staff, material resources and technical and educational aids.

9. Pedro Pablo Morcillo and Associates, 'Tasa de Valorización Obras de Infraestructura' (San José, August 1977).

10. We are indebted to Emilia Rodriguez at OFIPLAN for this diagram.

Index